BUILD A LIFE-LONG LOVE AFFAIR

BUILD A LIFE-LONG LOVE AFFAIR

Seven steps to revitalising your relationship

ANDREW G. MARSHALL

BLOOMSBURY
LONDON · BERLIN · NEW YORK · SYDNEY

To Ignacio Jarquin

Thank you for your support and patience.

First published in Great Britain 2011

Copyright © 2011 by Andrew G. Marshall

The moral right of the author has been asserted

Some of this material has appeared in a different context in *I Love You But I'm Not in Love With You*, which is also published by Bloomsbury.

Bloomsbury Publishing Plc
36 Soho Square
London W1D 3QY
Bloomsbury Publishing, London, New York and Berlin

ISBN 978 1 4088 0255 7

Typeset by Hewer Text UK Ltd, Edinburgh
Printed in Great Britain by Clays Limited, St Ives Plc

MIX
Paper from
responsible sources
FSC® C018072
FSC
www.fsc.org

www.bloomsbury.com/andrewgmarshall

Seven steps to revitalising your relationship

INTRODUCTION

Seven Steps is a series of books offering straight-forward advice for creating successful and fulfilling relationships. Getting the most out of love needs skills, and the good news is that these skills can be taught. If you have picked up this book, it is prob-ably because you want to improve your relation-ship. Maybe things have grown stale, the two of you have been taking each other for granted, or you have just emerged from a difficult patch and need to bond again. A lot of people think they have to 'work' harder or make grand gestures but this provides only a short-term boost. My aim is to help you develop good habits that will effortlessly transform your love not just today but stretching into the future.

Alternatively, if your relationship is ticking along well, this book will reinforce what is already working, help you avoid the traps that occur nat-urally as love changes over time, and sharpen up your relationship skills. Woven into every chapter, there are exercises to improve communication and boost intimacy. These can be done alone or, if you are working through this book with your partner, together.

In devising this programme, I have drawn on twenty-five years' experience working as a marital therapist. However, I have changed names, details and sometimes merged two or three of my clients' stories to protect their identity and confidentiality. In addition, I have used interviews with people not in counselling and letters written to my website. My thanks to everyone who has shared their experiences and made this book possible.

Andrew G. Marshall
www.andrewgmarshall.com

STEP 1

LIFTING THE LID

The most amazing part of falling in love is not only finding someone special in the crowd but also the promise that this feeling will last for ever. However, turning that promise into reality is often harder than we imagine. Somehow the pressure of earning a living, raising children together and the general adversity that life throws at us makes couples stop and doubt their love. In my marital therapy office, I hear the same debate over and over. One partner will say: 'It's not realistic to expect nothing but hearts and flowers' and the other person complains: 'But love has got to be more than picking up the kids, meals on the table and a great holiday from time to time.' So which side of the argument is right? My answer is both. It is possible to have a life-long love affair and still feel as strongly about your partner ten, twenty, thirty and, especially, forty years after first meeting.

The proof is some breakthrough research at Albert Einstein College of Medicine in New York. They recruited seventeen men and women who still passionately loved their partners after two decades of marriage. They showed them a picture of their beloved, scanned their brains and recorded which part of the brain lit up. Next they repeated the exercise but this time used people who'd recently fallen in love. Exactly the same part of the brain lit up. So how do these long-established couples still feel passionately about each other? Here we go back to the practical side of the debate in my office. Keeping a relationship on track requires more than flowers and sweet words – although these are a good start – it needs strength of character, a dash of good luck, plus many attributes that can be taught: good communication, balancing personal and couple needs, teamwork and a fulfilling sex life.

What is 'Love' Anyway?

Almost every popular song is about love, and half of all novels and films. We read about it or see it on the TV every day. Surely we should understand love and at the very least be able to define it. But this is where the confusion starts. We can love our mothers, our children, and our friends – even chocolate. When it comes to our partners, love can describe both the crazy, heady days at the beginning of a relationship and ten years later taking his or her hand, squeezing it and feeling sure of each other. Can one little word really cover so many different emotions? Dictionaries are not much help. They list almost two dozen definitions – including affection, fondness, caring, liking, concern, attraction, desire and infatuation, and we all instinctively agree that there is a huge gap between liking and complete infatuation. The problem is that we have one word for three very different emotions: the early days and honeymoon passion; the day-to-day intimacy with a long-term partner; and, finally, the protective instinct of a parent for a child or the bond with our own parents.

This confusion about love is particularly dangerous today because love has been elevated from one of the ingredients for a successful relationship into everything: the glue that binds us together. Previous generations might have stayed together for economic need, because of what the neighbours might say, or for the sake of the children, but we are no longer prepared to live in anything other than a passionate and fulfilling relationship. On the one hand, this is wonderful. Within a society fixated on working longer hours, being more productive and aiming higher, love remains a small beacon of happiness. But on the other hand, these new demands put a lot of strain on our relationships. So if our relationships are going to live or die by love, we need a pretty good idea of what love is and what sustains it. But when everything is going well, we tend to relax; we let love smooth over everyday problems and don't ask questions – almost as if letting in too much daylight will destroy the magic. I think this is one of our society's biggest mistakes and something that I seek to rectify in this book, but first we need a new vocabulary to talk about the different kinds of love.

In the mid-sixties the experimental psychologist Dorothy Tennov set out to understand what happens when someone falls in love, but was surprised how few of the founding fathers of her discipline had examined the phenomenon. Freud dismissed romantic love as merely the sexual urge blocked, while pioneering sexologist Havelock Ellis reduced these complicated emotions down to an equation: love = sex + friendship. Once again we instinctively know that falling in love is far more complicated. So Tennov interviewed some five hundred people in depth, and found – despite differences in age, sexuality and background – a startling similarity in how each respondent described their feelings during the early days of love. These are some of the most common descriptions of being in love:

- Intrusive thinking (you can't stop daydreaming about your beloved).
- An aching in the heart when the outcome is especially uncertain.
- Buoyancy, as if walking on air, if there is a chance of reciprocation.
- An acute sensitivity to any acts or thoughts that could be interpreted favourably (she wore that dress because she knows I like it; he hung back after the meeting so he could talk to me).
- A total inability to be interested in more than one person at a time.
- A fear of rejection and unsettling shyness in the presence of the beloved.
- Intensification of the feelings through adversity (at least up to a point).
- All other concerns fall into the background. (As a respondent told her: 'Problems, troubles,

inconveniences that normally have occupied my thoughts became unimportant.')

- A remarkable ability to emphasise what is truly admirable in the beloved and avoid dwelling on the negative – even to respond with a compassion for those negative qualities and transform them into positive attributes. (It doesn't matter that he is shy because I can enjoy bringing him out of his shell; she might have a temper but that shows how deeply she feels everything.)

- Despite all the potential for pain it is a 'supreme delight' and 'what makes life worth living'.

Not only do people all over the world experience almost exactly the same feelings in this early romantic phase, but also both men and women report the same intensity. To distinguish between these overwhelming emotions and the more settled ones of a long-term couple, each of whom is only too aware of the other's failings, Tennov coined a new term to describe this early phase of falling in love: Limerence.

The Joy of Limerence

The obsessive, intrusive nature of Limerence would be immediately recognised by Martin, a twenty-eight-year-old whom I counselled: 'I met her at a salsa class, the attraction was instant, and we ended up exchanging telephone numbers – even though I knew she was married. It was against everything I believed in, but I couldn't stop myself. It was impossible to work until we'd had our morning talk, I'd ache if she didn't call and even found myself "just happening" to walk down her road to stare through the window so I could picture where she made those surreptitious calls.' Twelve months later, when the affair had ended, Martin admitted that they came from totally different backgrounds and had little in common. He put the attraction down to 'lust', but most of the time the affair had been non-sexual. Tennov agrees: 'Sexual attraction is not "enough", to be sure. Selection standards for Limerence are, according to my informants, not identical to those by which "mere" sexual partners are evaluated and sex is seldom the main focus for Limerence. Unless the potential for sexual mating is felt to be there, however, the state described is not Limerence.' In essence, someone under the influence of Limerence wants to become 'one' with their beloved and therefore sex, the closest two people can physically get, has to be part of the package.

Limerence can come, as it did for Martin, when a sparkle of interest is returned and becomes what the French call a *coup de foudre* – a thunderbolt. Alternatively, Limerence can sneak up and, in retrospect, the moment is recognised as something very special. Anthony, a thirty-nine-year-old web designer, had been dating Tasha for several months. They were enjoying each other's company but Anthony had not seen her as 'the one' until a visit to an art exhibition: 'She was so wrapped up in the painting that she didn't realise I was watching. In that detached split second, I was overcome with tenderness. The vibrant greens and blues spilt from the painting on to Tasha. She had somehow joined the sun-tanned naked bodies from the canvas, the cool water and the reflections from the trees and the grass. All the natural colours of the scene had been heightened and exaggerated by the artist and I found myself being sucked into the painting too. My feelings were bolder and more colourful too – could that tenderness really be love?'

For other couples, a friendship can turn into something passionate when one half finally sees the other in a different light. Juliette and Edward, now in their forties, were at school together and shared an interest in music, but nothing more, until Edward's eighteenth birthday party: 'I don't know how, but all of a sudden I noticed Juliette as a woman. It sort of sneaked up on me – maybe it was her long, dark hair – but suddenly a light switched on: love at first sight, but several months later. I plucked up my courage and decided to kiss her, but I was very aware that she was a friend and worried about how she would take it. It felt odd and I remember a very quizzical look on Juliette's face as I leaned closer. Almost like she was saying "Do you know what you're doing?" No words – it was all in the eyes, but I hoped she understood, "Yes, I do."'

As hinted before, Limerence can be the source of as much unhappiness as pleasure. It is possible for the object of Limerence to remain a complete stranger, or someone we know but who is unaware of our feelings. Even under these barren circumstances Limerence can still grow and develop. Samantha was taking a language class and became obsessed with her teacher: 'The way his tanned muscles would ripple as he reached up to write on the flip-chart; the pattern of the springy black hairs on the back of his arms as he leaned across my desk to mark an exercise and how he'd push his fingers through this thick black hair. Even if he lived to be a hundred, you knew his hairline would never recede.'

Samantha began to develop a set of complicated scenarios for how a relationship could develop. 'My favourite involved my car breaking down after class and the recovery services unable to come for at least five hours, so he'd offer to take me home. Except that his car would break down in the middle of a forest – a strange detail as I lived in the city – and neither of us would have a mobile. Our only hope of rescue would be a passing car, but nobody comes along that deserted road. So we have to snuggle together for warmth.' In reality, Samantha was too shy to express her feelings and, in any case, her lecturer was married. Yet years later the smell of a school corridor – 'a strange combination of bleach, unwashed gym kit and chalk' – can bring back vivid memories for Samantha which are just as potent as those associated with real long-term relationships.

There are five stages to Limerence:
1. **Eyes meet.** Although the sexual attraction is not necessarily immediate, there is some 'admiration' of the beloved's physical qualities.

2. **Limerence kicks in.** Someone under Limerence will feel buoyant, elated and ironically free – not just from gravity, but emotionally unburdened as well. All these beautiful feelings are attributed to the beloved's fine qualities. This is probably the last opportunity to walk away.

3. **Limerence crystallises.** With evidence of reciprocation, either real or interpreted as such from the beloved, someone under Limerence experiences extreme pleasure, even euphoria. Tennov writes: 'Your thoughts are mainly occupied with considering and reconsidering what you may find attractive in the LO (Limerent Object), replaying events that have transpired between you and the LO, *and* appreciating qualities in yourself. It is at this point in *West Side Story* that Maria sings "I Feel Pretty".'

4. **Obstacles occur and the degree of involvement increases.** 'You reach the stage at which the reaction is almost impossible to dislodge,' says Tennov, 'either by your own act of will or by further evidence of LO's undesirable qualities. The doubt and increased intensity of Limerence undermine your former satisfaction with yourself. You acquire new clothes, change your hairstyle, and are receptive to any

suggestion to increase your own desirability in LO's eyes. You are inordinately fearful of rejection.'

5. **Mooning about, either in a joyful or a depressed state.** (Tennov's respondents were surprisingly willing to describe themselves as depressed. Forty-two per cent had been severely depressed about a love affair and seventeen per cent had even thought of committing suicide.) 'You prefer your fantasies to virtually any other activity,' writes Tennov, 'unless it is a) acting in ways that you believe will help you attain your limerent objective or b) actually being in the presence of LO.' A third option is talking endlessly about your beloved to friends. As all the popular songs about the broken-hearted attest, even being rejected or ignored does not dampen down the madness.

Tennov's respondents mentioned eye contact so often – 'the way she looked at me, or rather the way she rarely did' – that she believed the eyes rather than the heart to be the true organ of Limerence. Indeed research by social psychologists (Michael Argyle and Mark Cook) confirm the importance of eyes meeting across a crowded room. They found that when humans experience intensely pleasurable emotions our pupils dilate and become larger, which unconsciously and involuntarily betrays our feelings. What is more, a small increase in the secretion of the tear ducts causes the eyes to glisten, producing what Argyle and Cook call the 'shining eyes of love'.

When Harvard psychologist Zich Rubin conducted an experiment using sophisticated recording apparatus, he discovered that couples whose questionnaires indicated a greater intensity of love looked into each other's eyes for significantly longer than couples less in love. In fact, couples in love spend 75 per cent of the time, when they are talking, looking at each other – rather than the usual 30 to 60 per cent.

EYE CONTACT

In the early days of Limerence, to quote the writers of popular songs: 'I only have eyes for you' or 'I can't take my eyes off you'. However, once we have settled down and moved in together, there are countless other distractions from our partner's beautiful eyes: the television, the mobile phone, and our watches.

We could debate for ever: do we stop looking, really looking, at our partner and then the love fades, or does the love fade and then we stop looking? Certainly the Harvard psychologist who monitored the amount of eye contact between couples believes that staring into each other's eyes can trick the brain into releasing phenylethylamine – a natural amphetamine and one of the brain chemicals that make people fall in love.

How can you harness the power of eye contact?

- Attract your partner's attention, either by calling his or her name or by putting your hand on their shoulder. The second tactic is particularly effective as you can use gentle pressure to bring his or her head away from, for example, the computer screen, to look at you.
- Wait until you have your partner's full attention and he or she is looking into your eyes and wondering what is happening.
- Look into their eyes. It does not need to be for more than a second, just long enough so you really see each other.
- Give them a kiss on the lips.
- Your partner will be suspicious and probably ask something like: 'What do you want?'
- Just smile and walk away.
- Repeat this the next day.

If your partner asks about the kiss, don't be defensive ('Can't I even ask for a kiss?') or go on the attack ('I have to ask for a kiss because you never give me one'), just explain how you used to enjoy eye contact when you were first dating. Although at first this exercise will seem forced, before long it will be incorporated into your routines and become second nature.

So How Long Does True Limerence Last?

At the bottom end of the scale, Tennov found few full-blown cases that calmed down before six months had passed. In my opinion, the most frequent – as well as average – duration for Limerence is between eighteen months and three years. This fits with the findings of social biologist Cindy Hayman of Cornell University, who tracked three brain chemicals (dopamine, phenylethylamine and oxytocin) in five thousand subjects in thirty-seven different cultures and also found that the intense phase of attraction lasted somewhere between eighteen months and three years.

But once Limerence has faded, does it have to disappear completely? Certainly the crazy, obsessive, possessed side of Limerence cannot be recaptured, but the intense joy, walking on air and supreme delight elements can return though more as flashbacks than the sustained full-on early stages of Limerence. Often these flashes come after periods of adversity, for example: being separated from your partner while she was away on a course or during the reconciliation phase after he had an affair. According to Stendhal, a nineteenth-century French writer famous for his essays on love: 'The pleasures of love are always in proportion to the fear.' Many couples experience a burst of Limerence after an argument, especially during the 'making up' phase. Phil and Edina experienced a blast of returning Limerence after Phil crashed Edina's laptop, destroying a report she'd been writing. 'We both hate arguing but this row went round and round; even the next morning, we weren't really talking. I saw things my way and she saw them her way – and that was that,' says Phil. 'We were completely stuck. At lunchtime, we had to go off to a rendezvous. On the way to the car, she brushed her fingers gently across the back of my arm. It felt electric, a huge surge of joy, as I knew she didn't want to fight either. We could work this out. My heart leapt and I felt I floated down the street.'

Although resolving a conflict or returning from a long trip away can be the most effective way of re-experiencing Limerence, it is important to remember that neither the intense form of Limerence nor the associated biological attraction lasts for ever. We should not castigate ourselves if we no longer feel the same as at the beginning of the relationship. And maybe it is just as well. Would it really be practical to be forever thinking about our beloved – to the exclusion of everything else – or to be always shy around them and fearful of rejection? When people make serious errors of judgement, for example reckless affairs or inappropriate relationships, and later claim to be 'blinded by love', they are nearly always describing the effects of Limerence. In many ways, Limerence can be a curse as well as a pleasure.

INCORPORATING THE LESSONS OF LIMERENCE INTO EVERYDAY LIFE

In the early stages of Limerence, we are determined to find as many links between us and our beloved as we can. We imagine what he or she would make of the book we're reading, the scene we're witnessing, or the fortune or misfortune that is befalling us. We imagine how we will tell our beloved and look forward to how he or she will react. How different from the dull evening routine of many long-term couples: 'How was your day?' 'Fine.' End of conversation.

So to reintegrate this element of Limerence back into your relationship, look for events that can be stored up and shared in the evening with your partner. You could even write them down in a notebook, so as not to forget. There are two secrets to making these snippets interesting. First, look for the details that bring a story to life. Second, seek out events, opinions, characters that play to your partner's particular interests.

Often, when I do this exercise with couples, I find one partner has been editing their daily news. It can be for a variety of reasons: fear of boring their partner; to protect them from the unpleasantness of the daily business grind; simply to forget about minor irritations. All these reasons might be valid, but holding back will create a gulf between you and your partner. So make certain not to edit and instead, just as in the early stages of Limerence, make a full and frank disclosure.

Ultimately, everyone needs a witness to their life – without one we feel invisible, misunderstood and in the worst cases unloved. So listen attentively to your partner's news and ask questions to draw him or her out and show that you are truly interested.

So What Happens to 'Love' After Limerence?

Once again, the problem is how to define terms. Sometimes books and articles refer to 'mature love', which sounds very boring, or to 'deeper feelings', which seems to be condescending to Limerence – which, although not deep-rooted, is strongly held. Again we need another new word to explain this second kind of love; therefore I have coined the term Loving Attachment. This kind of love is not as flashy as Limerence, but it is just as beautiful: your partner stepping out of the bath on a Sunday morning and suddenly you seeing him or her from a new angle and being reminded of their beauty; watching your children together in the school play and sharing a look of complete pride; or spontaneously buying a bowl of hyacinths for your partner when you had only gone out for a paper.

So what is the difference between Loving Attachment and Limerence? Our culture's romantic myths of 'true love conquers all' and 'I'll love you no matter what' are all built on poets' and songwriters' experiences of Limerence. Although the magic brings us together and helps us over the first few obstacles, to achieve and sustain a relationship something more is needed: Loving Attachment. Perhaps one of the easiest ways to understand this type of love is to compare it with Limerence.

- Someone under the spell of Limerence is bound tightly to his or her beloved however well or badly he or she behaves. In the case of Samantha and her lecturer, as he was unaware of her feelings he virtually ignored her, but her attraction to him still stayed strong. In contrast, Loving Attachment needs to be fed or it will wither and die.
- While Limerence makes someone turn even their beloved's weaknesses into strengths, long-term couples, Loving Attachment couples, are only too aware of their partner's weaknesses.
- Finally, couples under the spell of Limerence do not care about practical matters such as earning a living – because they have 'their love to keep them warm'; a Loving Attachment couple tackle the complexities of life and its practical demands together.

Unfortunately, the myths about romantic love – and lack of knowledge about Limerence – make us believe that once we have found our partner, we can then relax; and that love will automatically bridge any problems. Even when overworked or preoccupied with the children, we imagine our partner will understand if he comes bottom of the list of priorities, or she will forgive us if we fail to complete that task for her. In the short term, Loving Attachment will survive this kind of neglect. But if consistently abused, a relationship will deteriorate.

'I feel taken for granted,' explained Antonia, in my office, while her husband, Jerry, shifted in his chair until he'd almost turned his back on her. 'As long as the house runs smoothly and the kids don't make too much noise, he ignores me. He comes home and turns on the TV or plays computer games with the boys. He doesn't actually talk to me – not about anything important.' This was too much for Jerry. He finally turned round and took her hand: 'But I love you. Isn't that enough?' He had assumed that their relationship worked in the same way as when they'd first met, when Limerence was at its height and their bond could survive, no matter what.

Most couples end up in my office because one partner feels that their love is not returned and has, over time, become detached – and this was the case with Antonia. We think that love ends because of some monstrous piece of bad behaviour but, more often, it decays gradually through a million minor hurts. In fact, Loving Attachment can never be taken for granted and, like anything precious, needs to be tended carefully.

What Feeds Loving Attachment?

For most people, the following list will be second nature. However, couples under stress will skimp or disregard these relationship necessities.

- **Listening.** (With full attention, nodding, asking questions – so the speaker knows he or she is truly being heard.)
- **Sharing.** (Feelings, snippets from your day or chores.)
- **Generosity.** (It can be with your time, doing a job for your partner that he or she does not like, or a small gift.)
- **Body contact.** (A cuddle on the sofa, stroking the back of your partner's arms or full sexual contact.)
- **Supporting.** (Watching your partner play sport, giving a compliment, babysitting while

he or she takes an adult education course, buying into their dreams.)

- **A shared sense of humour.** (Private jokes, messing about and general silliness are great ways of bonding.)
- **The extra mile.** (We appreciate most the gestures that are really tough for our partner – such as humouring our difficult mother or agreeing to that joint bank account.)

LOVING ATTACHMENT EXERCISE

Audit everything that happened yesterday between you and your partner.

- Start from when you woke up and make a list down one side of a piece of paper. A typical list would be: breakfast; got ready for work; kissed goodbye; phoned from work; ate supper together; talked about day; watched TV. At the weekend, it would be longer and more involved.
- Now look back over the list and ask: what, if anything, fed your Loving Attachment?
- Give yourself a tick beside anything positive on the list, but be certain the event has truly strengthened your bond. For example, a phone call to chat could be included, but not one to ask your partner to pick up something.

- Are there any other items that could be changed so that tomorrow they could be transformed into feeding Loving Attachment? For example, massaging her feet while you watch TV, or leaving some freshly squeezed orange juice on the kitchen worktop for when he comes down later.
- Could you add in an act of kindness tomorrow, like running her a bath or sending him a sexy text?
- Is there anything on the list that you wished you had not done? Often we conveniently forget our less loving acts, but write them down too. This will encourage you to be more patient tomorrow.

Here are some of the questions my clients ask about the Loving Attachment Audit.

Q. How long does it take to make a difference?

A. Changes do not happen overnight. But generally it takes couples three or four weeks to make a significant difference to their feelings about each other.

Q. If I'm fed up with my partner, shouldn't it be up to him or her to change?

A. When we're upset with someone, our natural instinct is to treat them less well. Guess what? They normally sink down to our level and the relationship becomes trapped in a negative circle. Why not lead by example and do something nice instead? Your partner might not immediately respond in kind, but before long he or she will feel better disposed and ready to return the favour. Miracle of miracles, you have set up a positive circle. It just takes somebody to make the first move. Why not you?

The Third Kind of Love

If Loving Attachment has been neglected, and a couple have detached, their 'love' turns into Affectionate Regard – which is very similar to what we feel for our parents, children, siblings and best friends. Affectionate Regard will make us care for someone; want the best for them; certainly not want to hurt them – but that person's destiny does not feel intertwined with ours – as with Loving Attachment.

So what is the difference between Affectionate Regard and Loving Attachment? While Loving Attachment needs to be nurtured to thrive, this third kind of love is seldom conditional and exists largely independently of how the recipient behaves. This is why the bond between parent and child can survive more dislocation and even neglect than the bond between partners. It is a sad truism that many children abused by their parents can still want a relationship with them and generally even the parents of murderers passionately defend their sons or daughters. Of course most parent–child relationships do not have to survive such extremes. But within even the happiest families, parents can put their children through grief that would not be acceptable from anybody else. Conversely, no matter how often our children disappoint or exasperate us, our Affectionate Regard for them endures.

The love for a close friend is also Affectionate Regard, as once again we 'let pass' behaviour from a friend that would be difficult to accept from a partner. A petty, but telling, example would be the friend who slurps his or her tea; this behaviour is mildly annoying when someone pops round, but living with him or her would quickly set your teeth on edge. In the same way, more serious character defects can be overlooked in friends; our lives are not so intertwined and we can either close our eyes to bad behaviour or simply see less of someone. This is why friendships ebb and flow but the Affectionate Regard remains.

Confusing Affectionate Regard with Loving Attachment can cause a lot of misery. This is what had happened in the case of Nick and Anna, a sales manager and teacher who are both in their late thirties. His relationship needs had not been met and he had become detached. 'We always go out with other couples,' he complained, and, almost in despair, asked his wife: 'When was the last time we went out just the two of us?' Anna saw things differently: 'But we still have fun: that time we all rented the cottage down in Devon – all those endless games of Monopoly. That game of strip Monopoly!' Nick couldn't disagree, but in his eyes their marriage had become like a warm bath – comfortable but not very exciting. Anna had not realised how bad things had become because she had misread the Affectionate Regard, left over from fifteen years of shared memories, as Loving Attachment. Indeed, Nick described their relationship as one between brother and sister. For him, the loss of the passion from the early Limerence was a particular let-down.

So why can Loving Attachment slip into Affectionate Regard? There are two main culprits: neglecting physical intimacy and not allowing each other to be different enough. Instead of being two individuals in a relationship, the partners become one amorphous couple and either one or both will complain about losing their identity. Here is one of the most difficult paradoxes about sustaining Loving Attachment. For a long-term relationship, rather than Limerence, we need to find enough similarities with our partner – either culturally, socially or emotionally – to make a connection, yet we need enough difference to stop the relationship stagnating. Often it is the friction of rubbing off each other's rough edges that provides the spark of passion. Look at all the great fictional characters we fall in love with at the cinema, theatre and in books. Rhett Butler and Scarlett O'Hara, Cathy and Heathcliff, Elizabeth Bennet and Mr Darcy, Romeo and Juliet. Not only are they all passionate in their relationships but also each half is very different from the other.

Summing Up

We consider falling in love, and sustaining love, as something magical and deliberately choose to shroud the process in mystery. While understanding how a magician saws a lady in half might spoil the illusion, understanding love lays down the foundations for a life-long affair with your partner.

IN A NUTSHELL:

- Your relationship is a living thing and needs to be fed, so that your love can not only grow but also thrive.
- Be careful about harking back to the beginning of your relationship. Although this can provide the warm glow of nostalgia, it is easy to forget the angst and obsession of Limerence and to downgrade the calmness and commitment of Loving Attachment.
- Arguments can be positive as they bring issues up to the surface and stop couples from becoming too alike and falling into Affectionate Regard.

STEP 2

DIAGNOSE POTENTIAL PROBLEMS

Love changes over time and there are different challenges at different points along the way. Unfortunately, most people have no idea what to expect and therefore cannot tell if their problems are something that arise naturally from that part of the journey or a fundamental flaw in their relationship. The closest we have to a map is the classic love story. Eyes meet across a crowded room, two people fall in love, get married and set up home together. But what comes after 'happily ever after'?

Our culture offers a few landmark events: engagement, wedding, christening – but not every couple can or wants to fit into this pattern. We need something more comprehensive; something that fits the experiences of every couple. This will not only allow us to compare ourselves with others and check whether we are 'normal' but also, more importantly, to look further ahead in the journey and head off any potential problems before they derail us.

Six Stages of a Relationship

My road map from the first tentative 'I love you' to a whole lifetime together has six stages, each of which has particular hurdles and lessons for keeping love alive. In some cases, couples will interpret issues that arise naturally when crossing from one stage to another as personal failure or even as 'falling out of love'. But, in reality, the Loving Attachment has moved into another phase and has been subtly changed. Other couples are simply stuck at one point on the journey or one partner has moved more quickly on to the next stage than the other, opening up a gap of different attitudes and expectations. This chapter examines each stage, explores when they happen, and looks at the skills to be acquired.

Stage one: Blending

In the first year to eighteen months into the relationship, the new lovers want nothing more than to be together. Dorothy Tennov writes:

'The goal for Limerence is not possession, but a kind of merging, a "oneness", the ecstatic bliss of mutual reciprocation.' There is nowhere that this is more tangible than in the bedroom, with couples at this stage reporting high sexual activity. Paula and Mark had been dating for three months when Paula admitted: 'We took to brushing each other's teeth and using the same toothbrush. I know it sounds disgusting but I think it's really sexy and has brought us even closer.' All differences are overlooked or ignored as two people blend into one.

Blending provides new experiences and an opportunity for self-improvement. If one half of the couple has a passion, for example, for opera, mountaineering, Egyptology or dog breeding, even if their new partner has previously had no interest in it, he or she will immerse himself or herself in the hobby. It might start as part of the process of sharing everything with the beloved but can build into a lifetime of enjoyment. 'Dating Paula I actually felt cleverer,' explained Mark, a twenty-nine-year-old who worked in IT. 'I hadn't been to university, I just learned on the job. Although Paula had a degree, she was so interested in everything about me that I gained enough confidence to speak up more at work.' Mark's experiences are typical; during Blending, partners appropriate desired qualities from each other and integrate them into their own personality.

The intensity of togetherness means that both halves feel that they understand their partner and are completely understood in return. When couples look back at this period, it seems full of magic and madness. In fact, humans need a bit of both, otherwise how could anyone trust a stranger enough to let him or her into their lives?

Most common problems:
- Each partner is frightened of upsetting the other and of love being withdrawn, so everything possible is done to avoid arguments.
- If there is a row, it feels like the end of the world. Unlike couples who have been together for years, couples in Blending have no experience of falling out with each other, disagreeing and making up again. Intellectually, Blending couples know it is possible to survive a fight but with no actual proof of living through one, they worry that any disagreement could be fatal.
- One partner holds back for fear of losing their identity.

Skills: Letting go

It is important to surrender to the feelings during Blending. On the one hand, Limerence helps a couple let down their barriers, but at the same time their rational head is forever warning: be careful. Relationships put two fundamental human instincts at war with each other. We all long to be close, to be understood, to hold or be held by another person; yet we also want to be in control, to be masters of our own destiny. Successful relationships strike a balance between these two needs. However, to start on the journey, especially as we grow older and more cynical, we need to trust and believe that this time it will be different.

GET IN TOUCH WITH YOUR INNER ADULT

New love can turn even the most self-assured adults into frightened teenagers again. This exercise aims to help you find the competent adult side of your personality again.

1. Down one side of a notebook make a list of the things you argued about in the first year of previous relationships.

2. Down the other side, fill in how you solved them. This will get you back in touch with your hard-earned life skills.

3. If you find it difficult to remember problems, here are a few suggested headings: money, washing-up, time apart, friends, childcare, tidiness and how often each of you initiates telephone calls.

4. Finally, think about how you can use these skills to solve today's problems. Remember, rows are vital for clearing the air and learning about each other's needs. When your head has seen that these issues can be solved, it will make it easy to let go and trust your heart.

Stage two: Nesting

During the second and possibly third year, the couple become more committed and decide to move in together. Sexual desire moves from perhaps three times a day to a more manageable level. Finally the couple are aware of things beyond the bedroom and creating a home together becomes a new dimension for expressing their love. This is where Loving Attachment begins.

But living together and decreasing levels of Limerence mean that issues suppressed during Blending come up to the surface. Previously, when visiting each other's places, it was easier to avoid arguments over 'who does what', but now these practical issues take centre stage.

'It just wasn't the same any more,' said Nina, who had been in a relationship with Nigel for a little under two years. 'I got really frightened that I was falling out of love. In some ways, that wasn't a bad thing as I was concentrating better at work – goodness knows what my colleagues must have thought when I'd spend half the day on the phone to Nigel.'

While the previous stage capitalises on the attraction and minimises the distractions, moving in together can highlight the differences. 'I thought Nina also wanted us to buy a place of our own, our own little corner,' said Nigel, 'but she thought paying off her student loan was more important. For the first time I looked at her and thought: do I really know this woman?'

Fortunately, instead of denying their different opinions or ignoring them, Nina and Nigel talked through and resolved their argument. 'We've agreed to buy a few pieces of really good furniture that we can take with us,' said Nigel. 'We're just putting a lick of paint over the worst bits of this rented flat,' added Nina. 'Nina's got a really good eye,' said Nigel. 'I know it's not much, but when we show our friends I really feel we've achieved something: this is us.' Unfortunately, some Nesting couples worry about their emerging differences – 'What's wrong with us?' is a typical cry. These couples, in particular, need reassurance that their relationship is not dying but moving into another phase.

Most common problems:
- Familiarity can breed annoyance – eccentricities have transformed themselves into nasty habits.
- Often rows centre round 'male' and 'female' roles in the house. No matter how modern a couple might be, moving in together can reawaken old role models from childhood.
- Arguments going round in circles without getting resolved.
- Long-term tracking by the University of Texas suggests eighteen months' to three years' courtship as the optimum period for a happy marriage. But some couples find commitment hard and deciding to live together is a big decision.
- Previously, during Blending, the couple only had eyes for each other but now friends and

family become important again. The return of these outside forces can cause tensions between the couple.

Skills: Arguing

Often the rows seem to be about petty things – such as whose responsibility it is to clean the bath or which colour to paint the bedroom – and some couples feel it is pointless to make a scene. However, this type of argument should not be avoided, partly because otherwise the issues will fester, but mainly because it provides an opportunity to practise settling disagreements. It is far better to learn on minor issues, where the stakes are low, than to wait until something major and unavoidable crops up.

NESTING: HOT-SEATING A DECISION

Moving in together is a big decision and many couples try and put it off for as long as possible. If you are having trouble taking the plunge, remember that relationships cannot stand still – they need to develop. The best way to deal with ambivalence is to 'hot-seat' the feelings.

- Normally we try and talk down our partner's fears. For every potential problem, we have an immediate answer. This might be a practical solution, reassurance ('Don't worry, I would never do that') or dismissal ('Don't be so stupid'). With this exercise, you not only listen to your partner's fears but also ask him or her to expand them and discuss all the 'what if's. Try questions like: What will be the consequences of moving in together? What other disadvantages are you worried about? What is the worst that could happen? What else? I call the exercise 'Hot-seating' because you become like a television interviewer and place your partner in the hot seat and, without judging him or her, gather as much information as possible.

- Don't be afraid of silence, while your partner thinks. As a counsellor, I find nodding my head encourages people to open up further. This actively shows that you are listening but does not interrupt someone's thought patterns. Don't be tempted to talk down the problems, just keep going with a fear until all the possibilities have been exhausted.

- Next, jot down a heading that encapsulates the fears (for example: lack of space) and move on to the next area. If the fears come out in a rush, write them all down and then tackle the 'what if' scenarios one by one.

- Once all the fears have been given a heading, you will begin to see which are the most important. After a fear has been named and is down on paper, my clients will often say: 'Actually, I'm not that bothered about that one.' So I cross it off the list. After listening to your partner's fears, identify the ones which you too share and add any different fears of your own.
- Once everything is out in the open, and we feel listened to, our fears are much more manageable. Now you are finally ready to look for possible solutions.

Stage three: Self-affirming

This stage occurs in the third or fourth year. Up to this point couples have always stressed their similarities – perhaps encouraging a partner to join in with a favourite hobby or even giving something up to spend more time together. However, during Self-affirming a couple have to feel confident enough to enjoy separate activities: to remember that there exists an 'I' as well as a 'we'. After all, it does not take two people to go to the DIY superstore and choose a hammer. Not only is it natural for the couple's individual traits, habits and characteristics to re-emerge but the relationship actually needs each partner's individuality to ensure growth.

An example of a couple who successfully negotiated the self-actualising skill of being independent and interdependent are Maya and Robin, who both have children from previous relationships. 'At the beginning, we'd only do stuff as a whole family,' explains Robin, 'but after a while I missed playing tennis and as both my son and Maya's boys were interested too, I started coaching them on Saturday mornings. I felt guilty when I suggested it because I didn't want to exclude Maya, but actually she was happy to take my daughter shopping. And it doesn't stop us all meeting up for lunch.' On the first week of the new arrangement, Maya was not so sure, but she was soon won over: 'It was stupid, really, to expect to be everything to each other. Robin doesn't like going to the theatre and there's really nothing to stop me going at the beginning of the week with one of my friends – and it's cheaper then.' Robin and Maya found other benefits too. 'Being apart gave us something to talk about when we met up later,' explained Robin.

During this stage, each partner has to balance what is in his or her best interests with what is in the best interests of the relationship. This can come as quite a shock, especially after Blending and Nesting, where the needs of the relationship have always come first. Some couples pretend their personal needs are not important, but this builds up long-term resentment and potential identity issues. Another problem during Self-affirming is one partner asserting their individual needs sooner than the other. This is often read as personal criticism – 'Why don't you want to spend time with me any more?' – rather than being a natural phenomenon of this relationship stage.

Most common problems:

- If one half has no clear idea of who they are, or has low self-esteem, it can seem more comfortable for them to hide in a couple identity than to re-establish their own parallel, separate identity.
- One partner can think the other's time alone is a threat to the partnership; or one partner will be unable to voice their independent personal needs.
- One partner tries to stop the other having personal time, for fear it will signal the end of the relationship.
- Power struggles emerge centre stage.

Skills: Compromise

If the squabbles during Nesting have been resolved, the couple find it easier to deal with the bigger issues that have been lurking behind the petty ones. During the first two stages, the basic human need to be close has been at the forefront. Now, with Self-affirming, the need to be in control of our destiny reasserts itself. So the couple remember their individual needs and begin negotiating about how much personal time is permissible. Often this can take hours and hours of discussion, and, particularly with smaller issues, this can be exhausting. Compromise is important; otherwise the balance will fall too much in one person's favour and ultimately undermine the relationship.

RELATIONSHIP BOARD MEETING

The following exercise will not only help separate individual from shared responsibilities but will also provide an opportunity for compromise – the main asset for Self-affirming.

1. On separate cards write down the major tasks and responsibilities that your life together generates. The list could include: money, social life, the car, the garden, cooking, food

shopping, decorating, insurance, paying bills, families, making large purchases, holidays, pets, household chores, laundry. Some couples like to include abstract ideas such as: fun, spontaneity, cuddles. The choice is up to you, but the more cards and the more detailed the better.

2. Each partner divides a piece of paper into three columns: me, you and us.

3. Next, each of you writes where you feel each task should go; afterwards, share your responses and the thinking behind them. Often you will simply agree on who does what, but often there will be a proviso – for example: one partner looks after the car but deciding on a replacement will be a joint responsibility. These provisos are an opportunity to clarify how far one partner's power extends.

4. Remember, compromises only work when there is something in it for both parties. So go back and check: does the division feel fair? Did one of you back down too quickly? Was one of you too ready to please? With genuine compromise, there are no winners and losers.

Here is an example of the Relationship Board Meeting in action. Emily took the card for 'social life': 'I've always made all the arrangements, even with Bob's parents.' However, she admitted: 'I've never been very good with money – and have no idea how to budget. Bob is very good, so I let him take over the standing orders, and working out how much we spend in different areas. It was rather a relief to stop worrying about it.' Bob was happy to take the card with these particular responsibilities. It soon became clear where each partner's strengths lay. The problems arose when either Bob or Emily felt they were not properly consulted in the other's areas of expertise. So we looked for a compromise. Emily consulted Bob about whether or not he wanted to go to a particular concert, but she made the bookings and checked if other friends wanted to join them. Bob consulted Emily about budgets but he made the arrangements – like consolidating their loans. The secret is to find a balance that plays to individual strengths but without undermining the loving bond.

Stage four: Collaborating

From approximately the fifth to the fourteenth year, couples use the security gained from within the relationship, and a greater sense of themselves gained from Self-affirming, to launch successful outside projects. It could be a career change, a further education course or simply new interests. This stage is called Collaborating because of the high degree of support the other partner gives. The excitement and freshness generated is brought back into the relationship and shared. Alternatively, the project can be a joint one – using complementary skills – and the most common choice is having children together. Couples who meet later in life may decide to launch a business or travel together. Whatever the joint or individual goal, it imports new things into the relationship and avoids stagnation.

During Collaborating, reliability and dependability replace the insecurity and fear of possible loss from the previous stages. Couples have earned their easy familiarity and have developed complementary skills around the house; they know how the other thinks and feels – but without the illusions of the first year. A shared shorthand, rather than the previous stage's hours of negotiation, is used for sorting out differences. Although this type of communication is time-effective, it can cause misunderstandings. If a couple are tired and stressed by children, one partner often needs extra reassurance. 'I sort of know that Miranda loves me,' said Don, 'but it wouldn't have hurt her to show me on a couple of occasions. When we first met, she had this funny business where she'd kiss different parts of my body and tell me that she loved them. It seems stupid to ask, but it would be so nice.' If this type of thinking is not dealt with, one half of the couple will feel isolated – like a housemate rather than a lover.

Most common problems:

- Taking each other for granted, or one partner growing up more quickly and therefore risking leaving the other behind – this is especially common for couples who met in their late teens and early twenties.
- If there is poor communication, one half of the couple can become too wrapped up in an outside project and neglect the other.
- There is a fine line between separate activities that enrich the relationship and those which leave the couple growing apart.
- This is probably the hardest stage of the six stages. It is, therefore, no surprise that the average duration for a failed marriage in the United Kingdom is 11.3 years (Source: Office for National Statistics, 2004).

Skills: Generosity

Previously, compatibility and common goals were the ingredients for a successful relationship. In these later stages, a lack of possessiveness is the key. It can be a difficult transition and especially hard when one partner launches into something new when the other is either not ready or has not found their own path. However, the extra distance helps couples keep their interest in each other alive and minimises the potential for boredom. Ultimately, couples at this stage have to be generous enough to bless each other's projects and believe that they will ultimately improve, not undermine, the relationship.

FINDING YOUR DREAM

If you have yet to find a project, either together or separately, this exercise should help. Before starting, it is important to understand the blocks to reaching your potential. Instead of fantasising about a potential project or interest and properly investigating the possibilities, many people immediately tell themselves one of the following:

- 'It's not practical.' Forget about the practicalities; anything is possible in dreams.

- 'It won't bring in any money.' Dreams feed your soul; express who you are; provide an interest so all-consuming that time just disappears. It could be taking an art course, building a model railway in the garden or getting down your golf handicap. Money does not come into it.
- 'I'm not talented enough.' First, dreams are about enjoying yourself, so whether you do something well, indifferently or badly is completely unimportant. If you enjoy it, keep on doing it. Second, researchers have found that anybody can reach professional standards in anything, no matter what their original aptitude. It just takes about ten thousand hours of practice. So who knows?

Having temporarily silenced your internal critic, you are now ready:

1. Find somewhere quiet so you won't be disturbed.
2. Close your eyes and imagine where you would like to live, then what work, what kind of relationship, what social life, what hobbies you would like to have.
3. Imagine all the details, so the fantasy seems as real as possible. Don't rule anything out as impossible until you've finished creating your perfect life.

4. Really fill in the pictures. What colours? What smells? What sounds?

5. Imagine a door in a room in your dream world, open it and enter into the dream. What more can you learn as you really immerse yourself?

6. Open your eyes and work out how to start realising your dream.

7. The next day, make a start: book the golf lessons, buy a book about watercolour painting or start measuring up your garden for a model railway track.

Stage five: Adapting

From fifteen to twenty-five years into the relationship, couples are busy adapting to the changes thrown at them, rather than dealing with internal changes within their relationship. These can be everything from children leaving home to ageing parents. By now each partner has given up the fantasy of what the other person might be and tends to think: 'He's always been like this and probably always will be' or 'What's the point of going on about her bad habits – actually, they're quite endearing.' Perversely, when someone stops trying to change us, and accepts us as we are, this is when we are most likely to bend. Couples at this stage feel contented; friendship and companionship are important. With increased self-confidence and less concern about what other people think, this is often a period of sexual reawakening. The frequency might not be as high as at the first stage, but the quality is much better.

An example of how two different outside pressures can impact on a couple is Nick and Anna, who we met in Chapter One. Nick felt extra responsibility for his mother following his father's death and therefore had less time for Anna. Meanwhile, Anna talked about what would happen when their two teenage boys went off to university and how empty the house would seem.

For Anna and Nick, looking at how their relationship had changed through the first five stages of love provided not just a fresh perspective but also a breakthrough in their counselling. Previously, Anna had always been upbeat, always focusing on the positives about the relationship. Concentrating on the challenges during the adapting stage, in her case the boys leaving home, Anna said: 'It's not just their physical presence, because they're always out, but the thought that it will be just the two of us. I feel all empty.' She turned to Nick: 'Just you and me, for Sunday lunch.' Now Nick felt she understood that real changes needed to be made in order to save their relationship.

The downside of accepting partners, warts and all, is that it makes change seem impossible. With this viewpoint, 'he or she has always been like this' quickly shifts from reassuring to depressing. Both men and women tell me: 'I want to feel special again.' However, by taking a fresh look, and with a little work, what seems stale and empty soon becomes warm with life again.

Most common problems:

- Couples can take each other for granted and become less expressive and less likely to show emotion.
- Although there are advantages to accepting each other's foibles, there is also a darker side. Some people assume that their partner is incapable of change and so ending the relationship seems the only option. (If this sounds familiar, read *Help Your Partner Say 'Yes'*, another title in this series.)
- Sometimes, during a crisis, one half might wish to retreat back to the safety of an earlier stage. Men who have been made redundant are compelled to start home improvements of the Nesting stage, or to want a return to the

closeness of Blending. Women who previously shouldered the majority of the caring – for children and elderly relatives – can return to Self-affirming.

- One partner will assume that the other has enough to worry about and will not confide their own problems.
- Sleeper problems begin to burst to the surface, reawakened by family events. For example: the death or serious illness of a parent can make someone reassess their childhood, with a knock-on effect to their relationship today. A couple's children reach the same age as when they first met, and thereby unwittingly bring back issues long since buried. However, these connections are difficult to spot, so couples need to keep talking rather than retreating into separate corners.

Skills: Listening

By this stage couples feel they know each other very well. However, major life changes – bereavement, milestone birthdays, and teenagers' traumas – can hit in entirely unpredictable ways. Adapting couples make assumptions about their partners' reactions and needs based on the past – not always the best predictor for the future. Therefore it is important to listen, really listen, both to what is being said and to what is being left unsaid. Some people try to solve their partner's problems but listening is more important, especially when someone is still absorbing the shock of change.

LISTENING SKILLS

Couples at this relationship stage think they know so much about their partners that they can even predict what they are going to say and may even have stopped actually listening.

Everybody thinks that they are good at listening – after all, it just involves a bit of concentration and not saying anything. Simple. Or is it? Two researchers recorded how long doctors let patients talk without interruption. The average time was just *eighteen* seconds. Remember, they knew they were being studied, so one would imagine that they were trying to show off their listening skills. When the doctors were presented with the research, two things happened. First, they insisted that they had let their patient talk for much more than eighteen seconds. Second, they claimed that if they listened without interruption, they would never get anything done, as the patients would talk endlessly. So the team did some follow-up research. This time the patients were allowed to talk for as long as they wished, without interruption. Most talked for only thirty seconds and no patient talked for more than ninety seconds. This research underlines how difficult it is to listen and the importance of this simple exercise:

1. Flip a coin to decide who goes first.
2. Partner number one can talk for as long as he or she likes about a current issue – without interruption.
3. To make certain that partner number two is really listening, rather than rehearsing their answer, he or she has to summarise the main points when partner number one has finished. Three examples of what your partner talked about will normally suffice.
4. Swap roles. Partner two talks while partner one listens.
5. Partner one summarises number two's views.
6. Repeat the above as many times as necessary.

Stage six: Renewing

Older couples who have been together from twenty-five years to fifty plus are often the most romantic and the closest. It is much more than an echo of the Limerence during Blending. Closeness at stage one was based on the promise of a future together. Now the bond is based on the reality of a lifetime together. Renewing partners stop looking outside the relationship and focus all their attention inside. In effect, they have come a full circle and begin reaping the benefits of the investment in their relationship. Shared memories and private jokes are very important for Renewing couples: 'Every night before I put the light out, I tell Martha that I love her,' says Iain, 'but she has to chip in that she loves me more than I love her. Maybe she's right – we've been through a lot together, and I've always known that I can count on her.' This sort of security is a real strength for a relationship.

However, when problems infect a relationship at this stage, the shame of not being able to resolve matters can be particularly undermining. Irene, who has been with her husband for thirty-seven years, says: 'It is hard at sixty-one to admit that I can't resolve these issues, and I'm embarrassed to talk about them.' Like many people with years of negotiating, agreeing to differ and pulling together, Irene still manages to be upbeat: 'I suppose every relationship is an ongoing work and can continue to evolve after so many years – maybe even more so with all this experience behind us.'

Most common problems:

- Sometimes, like at the Blending stage, these partners can be afraid to voice differences. In particular, when other people start encroaching on their time together – for example, children expecting too much help minding grandchildren.
- Health worries can isolate and turn closeness into claustrophobia. However, these are just minor difficulties for the relationship, and this stage can truly be called the best of times.

Skills: Patience

As we grow older, we seem to become a caricature of ourselves. For example, someone who might previously have been mildly worried about being late, starts doing dry runs of journeys to make certain that they know exactly how long it will take. Not surprisingly, this can also make us more difficult to live with. Therefore patience and understanding can be useful skills to negotiate a way through idiosyncrasies and to keep the worst in check.

SCULPTING YOUR RELATIONSHIP

Couples at this stage have known each other for so long that it is good to have a fresh perspective. This exercise also brings complex feelings up to the surface and helps put them into words. It can be done alone but it is better if completed with your partner.

1. Take a box of buttons or a pile of change and spread them out on a table.
2. If you are doing this with your partner, divide the tokens up so you have half each.
3. Without conferring, each person chooses one token to represent themselves, then one for their partner and each member of the family.
4. Now you are going to create a picture of your family with the buttons/coins.
5. Start with you and your partner. How close or how far apart should you put these tokens?
6. Don't think too much about where to put everything. Go with your instincts for the time being.
7. Next, move on to your family. Is your daughter closer to your partner than to you? Does she get in between you sometimes and therefore should she be sculpted in the middle? Does your son seem outside the family? What is the best way to show this?
8. Next, add in hobbies, pets, interests or jobs that make up part of your world. Where should these tokens be placed?

9. When you have finished adding everything, take a second look at your sculpture and check that everything is in the right place.

10. Share your thinking with your partner. Did you choose the token to represent yourself and your partner for any special reason? Explain what all the tokens symbolise and the reasons for placing them where you did.

11. Finally, if you could change one thing in both your own sculpture and your partner's, what would it be? How could you make this happen in reality?

12. Remember, an open mind and new ideas will allow your relationship to continue to grow.

What If I Don't Fit These Stages?

Generally, the first three stages work at whatever age someone meets their partner, and whether it is first love or love number ninety-nine. Stages four and five are of shorter duration for couples who meet later in life and for second marriages, while stage six is another universal experience. Remember that the Six Stages of a Relationship are a guide, not a prescription, so don't worry if you have not done everything in the right order.

For example, some couples have a child together (Stage four: Collaborating) before moving in together (Stage two: Nesting). Although this makes it harder to balance the independence and interdependence of a successful relationship (a crucial skill in Stage three: Self-affirming), most couples find a way of doing so. It makes for a bumpier ride, but then the potential for growth is even greater. Alternatively, when times are tough, you might find yourself retreating back to an earlier stage. A classic example is a couple who recommit to the relationship after one of them has an affair – they will spend several intense months Blending again, although this stage will be much shorter the second time round.

Summing Up

Relationships have a natural rhythm and each stage a natural season. Although every partnership is different, and subject to its own particular circumstances, following the general pattern makes life easier. More importantly, understanding the journey ahead allows you to diagnose potential problems and to head them off before they become serious.

IN A NUTSHELL:

- Trying to keep a relationship exactly the same for ever is not only impossible but also stores up problems for the future.
- Problems arise because people assume their partner will always have the same needs as at the start of the relationship; but life changes our expectations and us.
- Embrace change and learn from it.

STEP 3

IMPROVE YOUR
COMMUNICATION

If you wanted to communicate with someone Japanese, you'd probably hire an interpreter or study their language and culture. However, when we fall in love, we assume that our partner has exactly the same take on romance as we do. During the early days of a relationship – when Limerence is at its height – these differences don't matter. Our whole focus is on our beloved and, with this level of attention, we are almost guaranteed to hit their love language. The problem comes after the honeymoon phase, when realities – like earning a living – begin to intrude. At this point, we retreat into our main language with perhaps a little bit of a second language thrown in. There is no problem if this is our partner's take on love too, but here is the catch: I have identified five different languages of love. So what happens if you speak one language and your partner mainly speaks another?

Kathleen and Philip, a couple who sought my professional help, are a good example of this kind of miscommunication. Beneath some terrible rows, it was clear that they had a very special bond, but neither of them felt loved. When I asked how they showed they cared for each other, Kathleen explained that she spent the months before a birthday or Christmas scouring the shops for just the right gift, hid it in a secret place, then finally decorated the parcel with fancy ribbons. By contrast, Philip demonstrated his caring side with compliments about Kathleen's looks and by every day saying, 'I love you.' Both are equally good ways of expressing love. Except that here each partner secretly wanted the other to speak his or her own very particular love language. In consequence, Kathleen felt devastated when Philip gave her just a card and money to buy her own present; he was upset because she never whispered sweet nothings.

Sadly, we assume that our partner's love needs are exactly the same as ours. It is a natural assumption, but a deadly one. With other couples, one partner will be trying a multitude of ways to express love but still fail to get through. Alice, a forty-two-year-old wildlife conservation manager, was no longer in love with Jasper, her partner of seventeen years. Originally Jasper had pledged to do anything to rescue their relationship: he had started helping out more round the house, paid her more compliments, and generally tried to be more attentive. 'I didn't know love had to be such hard work,' he complained when he started counselling. To make matters worse, Alice was still not certain whether or not she loved him. 'I think she wants me to be somebody else,' said Jasper, 'and I don't know if I can be – or even want to be.' Not only was he failing to communicate his Loving Attachment, but also the effort involved was driving the couple further apart. The answer was not for Jasper to try harder – a scattergun approach – but for him to do less and target better.

Do You Both Speak the Same Language of Love?

Over the past twenty-five years I have observed many different ways of expressing love, but they seem to fall into five broad categories:

Creating quality time together

This can range from lying in each other's arms while watching TV through to exotic foreign holidays. These people can become fed up if their partner spends too much time on friends, hobbies or at work. Their most likely complaint would be: 'We never have any fun together' or 'You've got time for everybody but me.' The worst thing their partner could do would be to put off a 'date' or 'family day out' to catch up on chores or cancel because a friend needs them.

If this is your partner: The event is less important than spending time together, but a generous partner would choose an activity that gives their other half pleasure too. Even if the date involves something that you do not particularly enjoy, go along with good grace – as this will earn you even more plus points. During time together, make certain that you are truly focused on your partner and sharing not just your time, but your thoughts too. This could, for example, be a comment on the shared activity or something personal that has come up during the week.

Caring actions

Sometimes these can be basic partnership tasks such as earning a good salary or keeping a nice house, but normally they are more intimate: cooking a three-course meal, helping your partner clean out the shed or taking their sister to the airport at 3 a.m., for example. People who show their love through caring actions are most likely to say: 'Actions speak louder than words.' The worst thing their partner could do would be not to finish that little job as they had promised.

If this is your partner: The stakes have increased since the days when salary earning and house-keeping truly counted as caring actions, especially as work tends to be invisible to your partner and sadly a smooth-running house can be taken for granted. So look for the extra-special things that your partner might not even have thought about: taking the car to be valeted, installing some new anti-virus software on the home computer or baking a cake. These actions are especially appreciated if they are something you would not regularly do. If you are uncertain as to what might constitute a caring action in your partner's eyes, listen to what he or she complains about. At the moment, this will feel like being nagged, but look for a twist to turn it into a demonstration of your love. For example, the complaint might be a messy bathroom. Don't just tidy up, but buy small votive candles and run him or her a hot bath too.

Affectionate physical contact

Sex immediately springs to mind, but often the hugs and spontaneous kisses are more important. These people adore back rubs and massages and are most likely to say: 'Come here and give us a kiss.' Naturally, they can be devastated if their partner pushes them off because they're too busy doing something else.

If this is your partner: Affectionate physical contact works best when it is taken out of the sexual arena, as the power of an orgasm can overwhelm everything else. The hand in the small of your partner's back as you guide her through the door, stroking the back of his hand as you watch a movie together, or a kiss on the nape of the neck as you pass in the hall; all these are simple nonsexual ways of showing love. Feedback is particularly important for this language, so don't be afraid to ask which contacts were appreciated and which felt uncomfortable or ill-timed.

Appreciative words

If anybody is likely to write romantic poetry, it is this group. They want the whole world to know their partner is special by dedicating a song to 'the love of my life' at the local karaoke bar and placing sloppy adverts in the paper on Valentine's Day. They are most likely to say: 'I love you', and be upset by their partner brushing them off with 'You're just saying that . . .'

If this is your partner: Compliments are very important to these people and they want their partners to be cheerleaders, urging them on to even higher achievements. It is not just work, but chores about the house and arranging social events that need praise: 'Thank you for choosing such an interesting play' or 'You got a really smooth finish on the paintwork.' As well as the appreciative words, make certain that your body language matches. When you tell your partner: 'I love you', make certain that you are looking directly into his or her eyes. These partners also enjoy giving compliments. So make certain that you graciously accept them. It might be tempting to try and brush them away: 'It was nothing' or 'Isn't that what anybody would have done?' Instead go for the simplest and most effective response: 'Thank you.'

Present-giving

From an expensive piece of jewellery through to a chocolate bar bought on the way home, present-givers love to surprise their partner and will go to great lengths to pull off a stunt. They are most likely to say: 'I saw this and thought of you.' The worst thing their partner can do is to not appreciate the gift or dismiss it: 'I don't need one of those.'

If this is your partner: Gifts are an integral part of love and central to our marriage rituals. However, today's culture is obsessed with the value of presents and has forgotten their true message: 'This is something to say that I've been thinking about you.' Cutting an appropriate picture out of a magazine and making your own card can be a hundred times more effective than automatically buying the same old perfume. Don't wait, either, for a special occasion; lots of little presents will make these partners feel especially loved. What if you are not a natural present-giver? First, get advice, either from people who know your partner's tastes or from the shop assistant. Second, look at the type of gifts that he or she gives. This will provide clues for what make acceptable presents.

Love Languages in Action

Peter and Elaine had been together for two years. They both knew that something was not right but had been unwilling to confront the issues for fear of what they might discover. Finally, after a tense Christmas, Elaine complained that she did not feel loved. It all hinged on Peter's previous marriage – his wife had died five years earlier – and Elaine felt that although she didn't want to compete, she still played second fiddle. Peter kept on insisting that he loved her, but she complained: 'Actions speak louder than words; show me.' The more she talked, the more obvious it became that her love language was 'caring actions'. So I explained the concept to Peter and he went away thinking.

The couple returned the next week wreathed in smiles. 'I looked at my house afresh, through the eyes of someone who might feel excluded, and saw just how many photos of my first wife are up. At least one in every room, sometimes more, even in the bedroom,' said Peter. 'I don't need to see her face all the time, it's up here.' He pointed to his head. Peter had taken the photos from beside the bed and reduced the others until one remained in his study and one in the living room. This 'caring action' had really spoken to Elaine, who not only felt loved when she discovered his decision, but also replied in his love language: 'appreciative words'. 'I know it must have been hard for you,' she told him, 'but I really felt that you had understood me.'

Alice and Jasper, whom we met earlier, found love languages a breakthrough after several difficult weeks of counselling. Alice had repeatedly complained how little time they spent together. Jasper had countered that his job was very demanding and listed their recent trip to the cinema, a meal out and a summer holiday. When I brought up love languages, Jasper quickly spotted that 'quality time together' was Alice's language. So he turned up at her office, on a day when he was less busy, and took her out for lunch. When bringing work home was unavoidable, Jasper took breaks with Alice in front of the TV – whereas previously he would have played computer games in his home office. Alice began to feel truly loved: 'Emptying the washing machine and the other things he'd done were nice, but I really appreciated lunch. You should have seen the look on the other girls' faces when he walked me back to my desk.' Jasper had targeted his energy into Alice's most effective love language.

Kathleen and Philip, the other couple from the beginning of this chapter, also began to speak each other's love language. He started bringing home flowers and she finally started saying 'I love you' without being prompted. In fact it was Kathleen and Philip who introduced me to the concept of love languages. Twenty-five years ago, I had just started work as a couples' therapist and was making little headway with this couple until my supervisor – who seemed to have an intuitive grasp of my clients' problems – suggested asking about present-giving. My next session with Kathleen and Philip produced the breakthrough; I started using the idea with other couples and found other ways of expressing love.

How to Find Your Relationship's Love Language

Many people will immediately recognise their own premier love language. If you are unsure, try completing these two statements: 'I feel most loved when . . .' and 'I am most likely to complain that my partner never . . .' The second statement is particularly revealing, as what we complain about most is what we long for the most. For your partner's love language imagine how he or she would complete those statements. It is also useful to look at how your parents showed their love when you were growing up. Some people speak one love language because that is what they heard as children, while others long for what they never had. There is more about finding each other's love language and learning to speak it in the 'Love Cards' exercise below.

LOVE CARDS

Get a packet of index cards, or blank postcards, and write the title of one of the five languages on to one of the cards. Keep going until you have a complete set: 'creating quality time together'; 'caring actions'; 'affectionate physical contact'; 'appreciative words'; 'present-giving'. If you have another way of expressing love, which doesn't fit under these categories, make up another card. Next, create an identical set for your partner. A good tip is to use a different-coloured biro in case they get mixed up.

1. Find a good time

It's best not to introduce this exercise when there is a tense atmosphere, as it requires a certain amount of good faith.

2. Make it sound fun

Everyone dreads the phrase: 'We need to talk.' All too often we interpret this as: 'You need to listen while I complain.' Introduce the cards as a game or a puzzle 'to help us understand each other better'. You can also explain that it need not take long. I've had couples who completed the love cards in a few minutes; others have taken the whole session to talk through the implications. It's up to you.

3. Give your partner the cards

Ask him or her to spread them out on a table and then put them in order from the most important way of showing love to the least. While your partner is doing this, you can be ordering your love cards too. It can be off-putting if someone is watching you.

4. **Ask for examples**

It is tempting to comment on your partner's choices straight away, but first make certain you understand them. For example: if his or her number one is 'creating quality time together', ask which times he or she particularly enjoyed. You could also share one of your favourite 'quality' times and double-check that you both mean the same things. Go through each card and ask for more examples. Your partner might have problems thinking of an example for the bottom few; it can be hard for something we consider unimportant.

5. **Share your examples**

Now it is your turn to give examples for your love cards. Keep it positive. Remember, it's about what you like doing, not about what you don't want. Children respond best to compliments – so will your partner.

6. **Compare**

Discuss the order in which you have each placed the love languages. What are the differences and what are the similarities? If you have any ideas why one is particularly important to you share them – for example: 'I came from a family where nobody ever hugged so . . .' Don't worry if your priorities are very different, the next step will help tackle this.

7. **Learn to speak each other's language**
    Remember, the way we show love is also the way we like to receive it. So try and increase the number of times you speak your partner's favourite love language. This is particularly important if your partner has fallen out of love with you. Ask him or her: 'What one change could I make which you would particularly appreciate?' These tasks should be small and easily checked. For example, if your partner's top priority is 'creating quality time together', make a resolution to have one meal out together a month. Don't leave any loose ends – decide who books the table and the babysitter. For any changes to stick there have to be benefits for both of you. So ask for something small in your language too.

    If your relationship has been going through a rough patch, a helpful twist on this exercise is to rearrange the love cards into the order you would like in future. One couple I helped started with 'present-giving' as their first choice. They explained that this was the only love language that felt safe. When we looked at their ambitions for the future, 'present-giving' dropped down and 'affectionate physical contact' came towards the top of the pack.

Love Languages in Reverse

If your partner's love language is a fast track to rebuilding Loving Attachment, what happens if you slip up? Robert's love language was 'caring actions'. When his partner, Elizabeth, forgot to pick up the dry-cleaning, it became a big deal. He told her: 'This just shows that you don't care.' Elizabeth, whose language was 'creating quality time together', thought that he had got everything out of proportion. By not understanding Robert's love language, she had unintentionally insulted him – just as a foreigner in Japan with no knowledge of the culture would be considered impolite if they put a business card away without looking at it properly. These simple misunderstandings turn a potentially positive moment between a couple into a negative.

John Gottman, professor of psychology at the University of Washington, set up a special apartment as a laboratory to study couples. As his volunteers went through their 'natural' inter-actions, he would observe them and monitor biological changes as the couples discussed areas of conflict. He claims to be able to predict with 94 per cent accuracy who will be happily married, miserable or even divorced within four years. He found that with happy couples, positive atten-tion outweighs negative by a factor of five to one. In other words, for every criticism, there should be five compliments. For every time we let our partner down, there should be five times that we come through. Sadly, we imagine that one good deed will cancel out one bad; Gottman shows that our natural instincts are way off the mark.

This is why it is vital to target your partner's love language. First, it will help maximise the positive interaction and build Loving Attachment. Second, it will avoid unintentional negatives. Third, when you do need to 'make it up' with your partner, paying attention to each other's love language can often signpost the most appropriate approach.

THE LOVE LANGUAGE AUDIT

Ask yourself the following questions and pinpoint the last time you used each of the five love languages:

- When did I last take my partner out on a date?
- When did I last do some chore for my partner without having to be asked?
- When did I last touch my partner in a tender and loving way without it being a prelude to sex?
- When did I last give my partner a compliment?
- When did I last buy my partner a present without it being a birthday or other special occasion?

If the answer is in the last few days, give yourself a pat on the back; last week is good and last month is also fine. For the questions where the answer is longer than a month ago, or for those where you cannot remember, take these languages as a target to show your love in a new way.

What Stops People Communicating Effectively

It is not just love that is hard to communicate; some clients reach a point where almost everything is misinterpreted. These partners don't mean to cause offence – they even start choosing their words very carefully – but somehow they still end up with an atmosphere. So what is going wrong?

Martin and Jackie had a flare-up over Jackie not filling the car with petrol after she had used it. 'What did I do?' asked Martin. 'I just asked a simple question.' But Jackie had a very different take on the incident: 'He came at me, accusing, all guns blazing,' she explained at their next counselling session.

They had sniped at each other and spent an unpleasant evening, each at their end of the sofa, nursing very different interpretations of events. Jackie was convinced that he had been aggressive; Martin was convinced that she had taken offence over nothing at all.

A neutral observer would have been surprised that something so trivial could be so divisive. But the first thing to understand is that neither Martin nor Jackie is neutral. Each of them is viewing the row through their shared history, their past individual experiences which stretch back to their childhood, and, most crucially, a million and one assumptions. It is these assumptions that undermine good communication.

So when Martin and Jackie brought the incident to counselling, I asked them to replay the conversation but this time I would intervene and help them uncover their hidden assumptions. So Martin started:

'What I said was: "Why didn't you fill up the car after you used it?"'

Jackie was about to jump in but I stopped her. She would get her chance in a minute.

'Why was that important?' I asked.

'Filling it up in the morning takes time and there can often be a queue at the pump and those ten or fifteen minutes can make all the difference between being on time for work and getting stuck in the rush hour,' explained Martin.

'Did you know this, Jackie?' I asked.

'I knew that if he sets off too late, he gets caught in traffic,' said Jackie, 'but not about the queue at the pump.'

'I thought you knew how fine the timing can be. Five minutes can make all the difference,' replied Martin.

I had found assumption number one.

'It wouldn't matter so much,' continued Martin, 'if you'd told me when you got back, "Oh, by the way, the car is low on petrol", because I'd have set off earlier the next morning.'

'Have you ever told her that?' I asked.

Martin had to admit that he hadn't. He had sort of assumed that Jackie would know this alternative approach.

Assumption number two.

Next, I asked Jackie to rewind and replay her answer to Martin's question about the empty tank.

'I told him: "There's no need for you to have a go at me",' she said.

'You sounded quite upset. In what way do you think he was having a go?' I asked.

'He was accusing me of being lazy – not bothering to fill it up,' Jackie replied.

'Did you think Jackie was being lazy?' I asked Martin.

He shook his head.

Jackie had just assumed this accusation – assumption number three.

After a short discussion about her childhood, Jackie admitted that her father had been very critical and often complained about her not trying hard enough. He would start with a seemingly innocent question about what she'd been up to at school but would soon veer off into a lecture about applying herself.

Jackie acknowledged that her childhood makes her sensitive to criticism: 'Martin didn't ask about the car in the calm way he did just now in your office.'

'How did he say it?'

'It came out all aggressively.'

In fact, over 90 per cent of communication happens without words – and this is particularly the case when we are under stress. Martin's tone, hand gestures and delivery had given the words much more punch than he had intended.

Looking at how many assumptions underlie even a simple conversation and how our unconscious body language complicates matters further, it is a miracle that any couple communicates well. Normally love and goodwill smooth over any misunderstandings. With this mindset, the assumptions are all positive: she was probably rushing back to watch her favourite TV show; he must have had a hard day at work. By contrast, all Jackie's and Martin's assumptions had been negative. In fact, a partner becoming prickly over seemingly unimportant matters is often an early warning sign of trouble. So how can you stop hidden assumptions from clouding your communication?

The Three-part Statement

Assumptions happen because we fail to give our partners enough information. This is why the 'Three-part Statement' is so powerful.

I feel [x] when you [y] because [z].

In Martin's case it would have been:

I feel [annoyed] when you [don't fill up the car] because [I don't have time in the morning and can be late for work].

The beauty of the Three-part Statement is that it is so tightly targeted that there is no room for assumptions. Jackie knows exactly what Martin feels because he has told her. She has stopped relying on reading his body language and no longer *assumes* something worse than annoyed – such as angry – because he has told her what he is feeling. The 'when you' in the Three-part Statement keeps things specific. Jackie knows that it is only a particular behaviour that makes Martin feel this way – not her as a person. Third, she knows the exact reason and can see that there are no hidden moral judgements. Although the Three-part Statement will seem artificial at the beginning, like all these relationship skills, it will quickly become second nature.

HOW TO USE THE THREE-PART STATEMENT

In times of potential conflict, ambiguous remarks can become so loaded with hidden assumptions – from both the speaker and listener – that clear communication is almost impossible. The Three-part Statement is designed to get as much information as possible out in the open as quickly as possible and to limit the potential for pointless arguments.

Don't skip any of the parts or improvise, as the recipe works best when followed to the letter:

1. I feel. . . . .
2. When you . . . .
3. Because. . . . .

Very few people can automatically put their thoughts into a three-part formula. It takes practice.

- Think back to the last time you wanted to say something and it came out all wrong.
- Write down the frame above and fill in each part. For example: 'I feel *humiliated* when you *ignore me* because *I'm trying my best to change*.'
- Try and come up with four more examples from the past.

- Now think of something current that you need to communicate. It doesn't necessarily need to be to your partner – the three parts work well with sensitive teenagers and work colleagues too.
- Write down the framework and again finish off each part.
- Ask yourself: 'Is this statement clear; accurate; and do I need to add anything?' If so, make the necessary changes.
- Practise the finished statement a couple of times; this will help it flow naturally when you approach the other person.

The Joy of Arguing

When I introduce couples to this idea, they are either shocked or they laugh. Arguments have such a bad reputation that we can only see the downside. However, rows can be incredibly positive:

- They bring all the issues up to the surface.
- They help us realise what issues are truly important.
- They show our partner that we care enough

to take a risk (rather than sweeping everything under the carpet).

- The process of disagreeing, making up and finding a compromise is one of the most bonding things that a couple can do.
- Good arguments provide a model for our children on how to settle disputes.

These positives are only possible if you stick to the following rules:

- Deal with the problems as they come up, rather than letting them fester.
- Criticise the behaviour (please don't leave your shoes in the hall) rather than the person (you are thoughtless).
- Take one issue at a time.
- Listen to what your partner has to say and try and put yourself in his or her shoes. What part of their argument is valid?
- No name-calling.
- No pushing, shoving, throwing things or anything that makes your partner fearful.
- Do not walk away from an argument – unless you are about to break the previous rule. (If your rows have become physical, it is important to seek help before the problems become ingrained.)

There is more information about good communication in another book in this series: *Resolve Your Differences*.

Summing Up

There are five main ways of expressing love: creating quality time together, caring actions, affectionate physical contact, appreciative words and present-giving. Careful targeting prevents misunderstandings, unintended slights and channels energy into the most productive ways of communicating.

IN A NUTSHELL:

- When your partner does not respond, try a different love language.
- Poor communication happens when there are lots of hidden assumptions; try and bring them up to the surface.
- Don't keep ducking arguments. They often provide the breakthrough to solving a problem.

STEP 4

BOOST INTIMACY

Everybody favours intimacy; much like peace, holidays and bargains, we all want more. So why, then, does intimacy slip so easily out of our grip with the result that many couples have OK rather than great love lives? The usual excuse is that modern lifestyles are stressful and eat into quality time with our partners, but this is only part of the story. Intimacy has been made to equal sex – and nothing else. Much in the way that everybody has become obsessed with league tables, performance and delivery, we've shoehorned loving intimacy into targets too. Sex might be reducible to the statistics of 'how often' and 'how long', but intimacy is not so obliging. Plus, in all the sweaty passion of lovemaking, it is easy to imagine that we are genuinely close to our partner. Men are particularly guilty of confusing sex and intimacy, and will consider their marriage good even if the lovemaking is routine and unfulfilled. Yet even physically satisfying sex can leave both partners feeling isolated, lonely and secretly wondering whether things can ever improve.

Patrick is a twenty-nine-year-old teacher: 'My pleasure is giving Cathy pleasure.' There is nothing wrong with this, but Patrick had become so considerate that he was not honest about his own needs. 'I occasionally think of trying something slightly different – like making love in the shower – but I don't say anything. What might Cathy think?' They were so worried about upsetting each other – and so self-censoring of their needs – that their sex routine had become boring. Worse still, they were unable to talk about the problems, which were pushing them further and further apart.

So what is intimacy and how do we recapture it? Intimacy is made up of three main components: vulnerability, good verbal communication, and physical closeness (of which sex is probably only 30 per cent). Get these key ingredients in the right balance and you will always feel both loved and desired.

Vulnerability

This is all about being open and risking revealing something about yourself. Not surprisingly, it is also the hardest intimate quality to achieve. This is because our fear of getting hurt may be almost as strong as our desire for intimacy. So we hold back and build up our defences as an insurance policy against pain. In the early days of a relationship this 'one foot in, one foot out' approach makes sense. We imagine that it will get easier after marriage, but often we become even more scared. Our partners learn so much about our failings as well as our strengths from our new domestic, financial, and child-rearing life together that to share too much more can feel like being swallowed up. Also, if you know somebody well, rejection feels more personal and we step up the patrols round our defences.

Good Verbal Communication

Even couples who were good at communicating at the beginning of their relationship can find their skills evaporating. In the heady early days of love, we never stop talking and share our opinions on everything from shellfish to Shakespeare. Contrast this with the stress of everyday life when communication is cut down to the bare essentials – what time you're back, kids needing money for school – as we cross in the kitchen. Although this shorthand is very efficient, there is no space for the rich details that taught us so much during courtship. In the gaps, we start to make assumptions. We fail to notice that our partner's tastes have changed and our opinions need updating. Worse still, we can swallow our irritations for the sake of avoiding an argument and the smooth running of the household. The feelings do not disappear but turn to resentment and further distort good communication.

Physical Closeness

What about physical closeness? The casual touch on the arm as you make a point, stroking your neck as you watch TV, smooching, long cuddles. Sounds wonderful? These little gestures are just as important as sexual intercourse. But why do they disappear from so many marriages after the first flush of passion? Sadly, casual physical closeness is often seen as an overture to lovemaking, rather than a joy in its own right. So if one half is not in the mood – even though they might be enjoying the sensations of the moment – they turn away. After all, they know where it will lead. Very soon these couples get locked in the 'all or nothing' syndrome, where everything beyond a quick peck on the cheek is off-limits – unless of course you want full intercourse.

These problems are exacerbated for men and women over forty, who find themselves at very different stages with their sexuality. Women whose children are more independent are no longer so exhausted. They feel better, have more time for themselves and feel that their confidence is boosted. Men, on the other hand, are moving in the opposite direction. They are less confident about achieving arousal and will often stay over their side of the bed unless 100 per cent certain of delivering. Finally the intricacies of initiating lovemaking often need updating in long-term relationships. What seemed comfortable and safe ten years ago – the hand snaking across the bed – can now seem like you're being taken for granted.

Sexual activity – like love – changes as a couple move through the Six Stages of a Relationship (see Chapter Two). While Limerence is at its height, during Blending, couples report intense sexual excitement, high frequency and often lengthy lovemaking. One of the great pleasures is slowly exploring every inch of each other's bodies – almost as if each partner is claiming the other as his or her own. 'I almost wanted to climb into him,' explains Jackie, who we met in the previous chapter. 'We still joke that when we cuddle I will burrow into his armpit.' This intense sharing diminishes any potential sexual obstacles to almost the point of insignificance and is remembered as a golden period. For most couples this stage lays the foundation for a lifetime of emotional and physical intimacy.

During Nesting, there is a gradual decline in lovemaking. However, the increased knowledge of each other's likes and dislikes can act as compensation and there is generally plenty of non-genital caressing and stimulation. During Self-affirming, years three and four, sex is most likely to become an issue – especially for couples who have been unable to handle conflict. At this stage, different needs for affection begin to emerge but some couples find it easier to turn over and switch off the light than to talk. The unresolved anger does not disappear but instead builds a wall between the couple and shuts down the sexual libido. However, for couples who allow each other to be individuals during the Self-affirming stage, as well as being half of a relationship, the changes in the relationship create new interest. Each partner learns both to give and take in lovemaking and thereby avoid one party feeling permanently in debt to the other.

Collaborating, stage four, is a time of new activities and many couples start experimenting with their lovemaking too. However, this can also be a time when one or both parties feel exhausted – especially if the couple have children. 'I thought Sue never had time for me,' complained Cliff. 'Although I know it's not easy having a four-year-old and an eighteen-month-old, I feel I'm being constantly pushed away.' Over time, Cliff felt that he had been turned down so many times that he no longer felt attractive – despite Sue's reassurances that her refusal was not personal. A good tip for overcoming this problem is rather than saying no, to make an alternative suggestion. It worked for Cliff and Sue. 'I might not have fancied intercourse, but often I could really do with a back rub,' said Sue. 'Afterwards I would return the favour.' Alternatively, Sue learned to ask for a 'rain check' and the offer of making love at the weekend.

With Adapting, stage five, after fifteen to twenty-five years, couples report a decline in the frequency of lovemaking but conversely that the quality is better. However, some people have issues about the changes to their body, and their partner's, and about feeling desirable. I would recommend two approaches for this – hiding the offending bits or conversely emphasising them. A sex therapist friend gets women who feel very conscious of stretch marks or men sensitive about post-operation scars to actually colour them in. She finds that not only does this bring fun and play back into the relationship, always useful, but also afterwards, when the colour has been washed off (maybe together in the shower), the couples report that the marks were not so noticeable after all. For the opposite approach, the person with the bits that he or she feels are undesirable is given the opportunity to cover them up. This partner starts with the fabric of their choice – normally something quite thick – and over time, replaces it with something thinner. Normally, the couple move in stages until they end up with just a scarf as they make love; eventually the person with the issue will be ready to go naked again. However, the choice and timings are always up to him or her. This programme was designed to help women after a mastectomy but works well for anything that makes someone self-conscious.

The final relationship stage is Renewing. The urgency of orgasmic release is replaced by an increase in cuddling, holding and caressing. Older couples often have the highest level of peace and contentment.

PLEASURE PRINCIPLE

Many couples, who find lovemaking a chore rather than a joy, have lost sight of the full range of possibilities for pleasure. In the worst cases, life has become a very serious business – which almost excludes playfulness. For many others, pleasure is concentrated in one or two areas, and the effectiveness blunted by repetition.

1. Think about everything that gives you a warm buzz/real pleasure and write it down. Keep adding to the list – nothing is too trivial. In the film *Manhattan*, Woody Allen's character lists the things that make life worth living as: 'Groucho Marx, Willie Mays [American basketball legend], the second movement of the 'Jupiter' Symphony, Louis Armstrong's recording of 'Potato Head Blues', Swedish movies, Frank Sinatra, Marlon Brando, the crabs at Sam Wo's and Tracy's face.' What would be on yours?

2. Look at your list and decide which of the following categories of pleasure, in your opinion, each item falls under. I have listed a few examples to get you going, but they are not definitive. For one person, a holiday will be an escape but for another, it would be a source of tranquillity and for a third, who might kayak white-water rapids, a source of achievement.

Achievement: Passing an exam, negotiating a discount, finding the perfect pair of shoes, closing a deal at work.

Tranquillity: A beautiful view, watching the water lap at the side of a boat, lying in a warm bed on a cold morning.

Irresponsibility: Putting your feet up for five minutes and reading a magazine, a quick round of golf, making shadow puppets at the movies.

Excitement: Driving a fast car, horse riding on the beach, scoring a goal.

Sensual: Roast spring lamb with mint sauce and new potatoes, listening to Leonard Cohen, the smell of freshly roasted coffee.

Escapism: Getting silly drunk, meditation, dancing, buying a lottery ticket.

Nurturing: Watching a child sleep, doing

some voluntary work, introducing a friend to a really good book.

3. The great thing about lovemaking/intimacy is that this provides one of the few forums that can offer all these pleasures at the same time. But how balanced is your list? Do all your pleasures cluster together under one or two headings? How many of the pleasures are shared with your partner?

4. Generally, couples without enough intimacy in their lives have both lost sight of **irresponsibility** and although each partner might have **excitement** and **tranquillity**, they no longer share these pleasures together.

5. Here are some ideas, under each heading, which are a pleasure to share together – **away from the bedroom**. What others ideas can you come up with?

   Achievement: Go on a five-mile walk together or landscape the garden.
   Tranquillity: Go to the beach and skim stones across the waves together, find somewhere to play Poohsticks.

Irresponsibility: Generally any forgotten child-hood pleasures like pushing each other on the park swings or running down a hill singing 'Jack and Jill' together.

Excitement: Visiting a theme park and going on a white-knuckle ride together, going to the races.

Sensual: Going to a concert together, filling the house with fragrant flowers.

Escapism: A weekend away or learning to salsa together.

Nurturing: Planning a special day out for your partner or cooking a favourite meal.

6. Sharing different pleasures will rebalance your intimacy away from the sexual arena; now it's time to bring the fun into the bedroom. This next game can be as sexy as you wish to make it – I call it: What have I got in my hand?

   • Each partner finds an ordinary house-hold item that has the possibility of being sensuous: a small paintbrush, a silk scarf, a pot of strawberry yoghurt, skin cream, or an ice cube. Do not tell each other what you've found – in fact, you might like to tease your partner about the possibilities, as anticipation is part of the fun.

- In the bedroom, each partner strips down to underwear and flips a coin to decide who goes first.
- One partner closes his or her eyes, while the other gets out their secret item.
- Slowly, gently, the person with the secret item moves it across their partner's exposed skin.
- The partner with the closed eyes takes a few minutes to become accustomed to the sensations; meanwhile, the other person finds different ways to caress them. Really get into the possibilities and find new places and new ways to touch. (The only thing off-limits is playing in a sadistic way.) How could you confuse? How could you give pleasure? However, please avoid the obvious erogenous zones for now.
- After at least five minutes have passed, the person with the secret item asks: What have I got in my hand? The person being touched can either guess or ask questions – (Is it something found in the kitchen?) – but he or she cannot open their eyes.
- After the touched partner has guessed correctly or given in, he or she can choose to continue to be touched or ask to switch over and the game starts again.

How to Fancy Your Partner Again

At the movies and on TV couples are always having passionate and exciting sex, but reality can be very different. In the landmark *Sex in America* study, one in three women and one in seven men were reported to have little interest in love-making. When married couples were asked to look back over the whole of their relationship, 50 per cent reported that at some point one partner had lost interest in sexual intercourse. So how do you relight the fires of passion?

The first step is to understand that this is not an uncommon problem. In sexual therapy, a low-sex relationship is defined as making love only every other week and affects 35 per cent of married couples. A no-sex marriage (which is not total abstinence, but intercourse less than ten times a year) affects 20 per cent of married couples. A typical couple are Maddy and Scott, in their late thirties, who have been together for ten years and have two small children. 'We used to have such a great love life. I'd pick him up from the station on a Friday night and I'd almost be tingling with anticipation,' Maddy reminisces. 'We'd make long, slow love on Sunday mornings and even be known to go back to bed in the afternoon for a cuddle. I loved the way the sun would stream through the curtains on to his naked torso.' She expected it to be even better when they lived together, but first their love-making dropped in frequency and then it became boring. 'It now seems to be the last thing on our minds – we're either too tired or I think: OK, let's get it over with.'

Sex is easy at the beginning of a relationship. Pure lust helps us over any general inhibitions and hang-ups – like messages from the Church or our parents that 'sex is dirty'. During Blending, two separate individuals become a couple, but to achieve this they have to lower their defences, and what better way than sex? Unfortunately, the ease of early lovemaking and the Hollywood/romantic novel myth of being swept away by our feelings, stops us from understanding how we move from the mundane reality of being a couple – nappies, laundry, bills – into the bliss of sex. That's why it is so important to be aware of the four phases of good lovemaking:

- **Desire** (positive anticipation and feeling that you deserve sexual pleasure)
- **Arousal** (being receptive and responsive to touching and intimate stimulation)

- **Orgasm** (letting go and allowing arousal to naturally culminate in pleasure)
- **Satisfaction** (feeling emotionally and physically bonded after a sexual experience)

At the beginning of the relationship lust almost hard-wires us into arousal stage, so we don't need to be aware of desire and how to feed it. We just magically fall into each other's arms. By the time the honeymoon period finishes, most couples have found other bridges from day-to-day life into the desire stage. But the couples who depend on just lust and Limerence are left stranded, frustrated and blaming each other.

Casual touching

The most important bridge to desire is 'casual touching', for example: holding hands in the street, a neck massage while watching TV or your partner nibbling your ear. This is the bedrock for a healthy love life. Sadly, Maddy and Scott had stopped everything beyond a quick peck on the cheek for hello or goodbye. 'The only time Scott tried to touch me was when he wanted sex. I needed to be nurtured, not propositioned,' Maddy explained. Scott might have seen his casual touching as an invitation to get close, but Maddy read it as demanding sex: 'I'd go all cold inside and push him off because I felt taken for granted.' They had fallen into that classic low-sex trap: all or nothing. They either had full intercourse or did not touch at all. To unpick the idea that a cuddle on the sofa was agreeing to making love, I set up a series of tasks where Maddy and Scott would spend time kissing and fondling but other more intimate touching and intercourse were banned.

A week later, they came back all smiles. 'I really enjoyed having the pressure taken off,' said Maddy. 'I could just enjoy the cuddle without worrying about where it was leading.' Previously, Maddy would have had to decide if she was aroused the moment Scott first touched her – which seldom happened unless she had had a few drinks – but now they had a proper bridge to desire. They could either enjoy the non-demanding touching, which is pleasurable in its own right – or decide to have sex.

Planning

While every couple enjoys the first bridge from everyday life into lovemaking, the next one is always more controversial. When I tried to convince Adam and Hannah, in their late twenties, that sex needs to be planned ahead – like any activity – Hannah sighed: 'It's better when it's spontaneous and natural.' I agree, but those qualities alone cannot sustain desire. Adam was more pragmatic: 'Remember when I got those tickets for U2 in concert? We looked forward to that for ages and somehow it made the evening even better.' Indeed, anticipation is important for building desire. After probing further into Hannah's worries about a 'sex date', she asked: 'But what if I'm not in the mood?' This is important because feeling obliged is a barrier, rather than a bridge, to desire. Fortunately, they had started non-demanding touching and Adam agreed that this would be enough intimacy if Hannah did not want to go further. Ultimately, planning ahead was a success.

'We stayed in and I cooked us a nice meal. Adam had put on some music and we danced in the living room and one thing led to another. Actually, it felt quite natural,' explained Hannah. For couples who feel self-conscious about planning ahead, I often include another 'bridge': play. When we were children, play was at the centre of our lives and a gateway to learning, team-building and an opportunity to let off steam: all of these qualities are just as important for good lovemaking. Unfortunately, as adults we forget how creative – and how much fun – playing can be. So I've had couples building dams across streams, having food fights and playing on children's swings together. These games break down barriers between couples, they see their partners in a new light and this is ultimately very sexy.

Balancing closeness and distance

The next bridge from the practical into the passionate is a surprise to most couples: good lovemaking needs distance as much as closeness. Charlotte and Edward, in their fifties, had not made love for over six months and described themselves as best friends. 'I always know what Edward is thinking,' claimed Charlotte. 'She's right; she does,' Edward agreed. They did lots of things as a couple – fine dining, a busy social life – but very little apart. 'We hold hands when we go shopping and he's very considerate – opening doors – but I wish . . .' Charlotte drifted into a sad silence. 'There are more important things in a marriage,' Edward chipped in. I doubt that's what Charlotte meant but she smiled in agreement. Instead of being two individuals, albeit in a relationship, they had become one amorphous couple – frightened of allowing each other to be different.

The first step was to encourage them to argue more – the quickest and most effective way to release submerged passion. Next, I asked them to witness each other's separate lives. Edward went to a conference where Charlotte was speaking. Charlotte watched Edward play tennis – an interest he'd given up when their children were young. 'I admired how he really went for each shot and he looked quite sexy in his shorts too,' Charlotte said, laughing. 'And I saw the respect of Charlotte's colleagues,' explained Edward. 'It was like looking through fresh eyes.' Soon after these visits, Charlotte and Edward reported passionate lovemaking again.

It is when we see the distance between ourselves and our partner, and recognise them as a separate person independent of us, that there is enough space for desire to return.

Fantasy

Another important bridge to desire is fantasy. Some people feel guilty daydreaming about a gorgeous stranger or a famous face from the TV;

however, 75 per cent of men and 50 per cent of women use fantasy to build anticipation. Next time you see a handsome man, for example, in the supermarket, allow the daydream to simmer and bring the fantasy home to act as a bridge into lovemaking with your partner. When the fantasy is about settings or situations, don't be shy about making requests for a particular turn-on.

However, be wary of making a full disclosure about fantasy figures – especially if it will cause jealousy. You are entitled to private space in your head, as this promotes the distance necessary for good lovemaking. If you find yourself consistently fantasising about someone at work or a friend, this is probably an alarm bell that something is wrong with your relationship.

Although not every bridge to desire appeals to everybody – see the exercise on the next page for more ideas – try to incorporate as many as possible into your relationship. This is the best guarantee for keeping lovemaking fresh. If all the bridges leave you cold, there are probably some obstacles to desire that need to be discussed with your partner. These include unvoiced anger, one half pushing for sex, over-scheduling, not enough time away from the kids, and worrying about sexual performance.

FIVE TYPES OF BRIDGES TO DESIRE

Relying on the same old comfortable bridge will eventually turn even the most passionate love-making into functional but unappealing sex. How many more bridges could you add to your love life?

Romantic: Dressing up and going out, dancing, satin sheets.

Erotic: Watching yourself making love in a mirror, sharing pornography, lingerie.

Location: In the shower, four-poster bed, cheap motel, blanket on the ground.

Sensual: Massages, cuddling on the sofa semi-clothed, long and lingering kisses.

External: Sharing gourmet snacks in the bedroom, adult toys, fantasy.

Five Top Tips for Communicating About Sex

If you find sex a difficult subject, the following points will help you overcome your embarrassment:

- **Don't talk about problems in the bedroom.** An immediate post-mortem seems like a comment on performance rather than an invitation to find out what is wrong.

- **Turn it into a positive.** Tell him: 'I love it when you're gentle', rather than, 'Why do you have to be so rough?'

- **Use touch as well as words.** Guide her hands to where you like to be touched; telling can seem like an order rather than a request.

- **Work as an intimate team.** A turned-on partner is the best aphrodisiac of all.

- **Take responsibility for your own pleasure.** Don't expect your partner to second-guess what turns you on, help him or her out. If you are unsure, experiment on your own.

TWELVE STOPS ON THE ROAD TO INTIMACY

These are designed to be done one per week, but stay at each stop until you feel comfortable. If you wish to move more quickly – that's fine too. However, just as intimacy normally bleeds slowly out of a relationship, it is best reintroduced gradually. Hopefully, the earlier stops will become second nature, so they are continued – without thinking – even while you are focusing on the later ones.

This programme is easier shared with your partner but do not worry if he or she takes any discussion as an attack, as you can instigate the Twelve Stops on the Road to Intimacy on your own. Your changed behaviour will lead by example and create a knock-on effect.

1. **Validate each other.** Compliment or congratulate your partner on a job well done. He or she will probably think you are after something, but just smile and repeat the praise.

2. **Grab opportunities to talk.** Think back to how detailed your stories were when you were courting. Everything is in the detail, for it brings the story to life. Ask your partner to explain something from their life too.

3. **Set aside quality talking time.** Every couple should take stock about what they want from life from time to time: Where are we heading? What are our unfulfilled aspirations? Be vulnerable and really open up about your hopes and fears too. However, the main aim is setting aside enough time for the two of you. We cannot be intimate if our relationship is nothing more than scraps left over from work, family and friends. Guard this time jealously.

4. **Confide a secret.** You might tell friends every-thing, but are you as candid with your partner? Choose something revealing about yourself to tell him or her. Do not worry if you seem to be doing all the confessing. Like sitting on a see-saw, your actions mean your partner will move too and over time become more candid.

5. **Touch your partner.** Reintroduce casual touching into your relationship. Stroke the back of your partner's hand when you're sitting down together, hold hands while she is watching TV, give him a kiss on the back of his neck when he is on the computer. Sometimes a touch is worth a thousand words.

6. **Share.** Take one bowl of ice cream and two spoons into a warm bath. Couples normally laugh when I suggest this one but they love it. Make certain there is only one bowl – because, after all, this is about sharing. Try feeding each other too as this can be very sensual. Feel free to make love, but remember this is also about being naked together without being obliged to have intercourse.

7. **Set the scene.** Take a long hard look at your bedroom. Is it a passion killer? When I've asked couples to describe where they make love, I've heard about everything from stacks of bills

beside the bed to animals sleeping under the duvet. Have a clear-out – the bedroom should be a stage for your passion, not a dumping ground. Make certain the room is warm enough, the lighting kind (candles are a good tip) and that there is a lock on the door. Finally, add a sound system to set the mood and to prevent worries about being overheard.

8. **Slow down your lovemaking.** Intimacy needs time. Unfortunately, men often head straight for the genitals and women sometimes want to get things over with as quickly as possible. As we hurtle down the highway, intimacy is left on the hard shoulder. Avoid the temptation to say anything about this during lovemaking. However nicely put, the comments will still be heard as criticism. Instead, slide his or her hands to somewhere else you would like to be touched. Add a positive affirmation: 'I love it when you . . .' Another way of slowing down is to change position. For example, the woman being on top allows her to decide the moment of penetration.

9. **Find new erogenous zones.** Where are our erogenous zones? Answer: anywhere where the skin is thin and the nerves are therefore near the surface. The middle of your back, the

underside of your wrists, elbows, the nape of your neck, the outer part of your lips – this is why nibbling can be more passionate than plain kissing.

10. **Skip intercourse.** Sexual intimacy is a whole body experience and intercourse should be an optional extra. Once you can be close without full-blown penetration, the stakes are nowhere near so high. Although you might not be in the mood for penetrating or penetration, you are seldom too tired to cuddle or be stroked.

11. **Make initiation a shared responsibility.** The person who always asks or sets the ball rolling for lovemaking risks feeling taken for granted or, worse, being rejected and feeling undesirable. If you seldom take charge, now is your opportunity. If it is normally your responsibility, hold back and give your partner space to initiate.

12. **Experiment.** Try bringing something new into your relationship. It might be somewhere new to make love, like the back seat of your car down lovers' lane, or something different like one of you keeping your clothes on while the other is totally naked. They don't need to be big changes, but something to show each other that you've made intimacy a continuing priority.

Intimacy Repair

When sex is good, but more a physical release than an emotional connection, try staying awake for five minutes after having an orgasm. I know this is tough for men who often like to drift off to sleep after making love. However, pillow talk is a wonderful opportunity to connect. Some couples use the warmth and security of post-lovemaking to give their partner a few compliments, but others talk in ways that would be impossible at any other time. I had one client who was locked in a toilet as a child and subsequently suffered from mild claustrophobia. She told her husband that in the missionary position it brought flashbacks of being shut in – especially when he collapsed on to her at the end of their lovemaking. He, of course, had no idea and promptly suggested trying different positions. Subsequently, their intimacy went from strength to strength but without the post-lovemaking closeness this conversation would have been impossible.

Summing Up

The most common cause of boredom in bed is a lack of intimacy. Little by little, without either partner intending it, sex can sink to the lowest common denominator: what is easy or what both do not mind. The challenge is to keep rediscovering what both partners truly enjoy.

> ## IN A NUTSHELL:
> - Find new ways of expressing intimacy. Variety stimulates the pleasure centres of the brain.
> - Be playful and laugh together. This strategy reconnects us to our childish sense of creativity and combats boredom.
> - Slow down your lovemaking and indulge all five senses.

STEP 5

BALANCING
YOU AND ME

What is the secret of a happy long-term relationship? The *International Journal of Ageing and Human Development* asked fifty couples who had been married for fifty-five years or more what they valued most in their relationship. At first glance, the results seem contradictory. Besides the qualities that you would expect, such as commitment, companionship and caring, there was a fourth one: independence. How do these couples reconcile commitment and companionship with independence? This paradox is at the centre of every relationship: we need enough togetherness for a relationship to thrive but both partners need enough individual space to be themselves. Respecting your needs, your partner's needs and your relationship's needs is difficult, especially as the right balance is forever shifting.

Does Loving You Stop Me From Being Myself?

Over time, partners in a relationship become more and more like each other. It is only natural that one partner's tastes will influence the other and that living together will file away the rough edges of each half's personality. This gradual fitting together generally makes for a more peaceful coexistence. However, some couples take this a stage further and become too alike. Why should this be a problem?

First, as discussed previously, difference provides the spark that keeps love alive. Second, too alike can become suffocating. Indeed, some couples grow as similar as two peas in a pod and frequently one half complains that he or she has lost their identity. Worse still, for the health of the relationship, this partner ends up believing that the other is stifling their personality.

Stacey arrived in my counselling office in tears. She was twenty-five, but had been with her partner from the age of eighteen, and was now finding the relationship so claustrophobic that she spent as much time away from home as possible. Her main complaint was that the relationship stopped her from being herself: 'I don't know who I am. I've lost myself,' she said, and started crying again. 'That's why I've just got to leave him,' she explained.

From Stacey's account, I expected to meet a controlling partner. Carl joined us for the next session and he could not have been more accommodating: 'Did I say anything about you going out? In fact, I'm not stopping you doing anything.' Stacey did not answer but seemed to retreat into herself. She had turned into an entirely different woman from the one I had met before. 'What is it that you want?' Carl asked. There was a long silence. Finally Stacey said: 'I can't be the person that you want me to be.' It was Carl's turn to close up. 'Now I've hurt him,' Stacey said, starting to cry. 'I didn't want to do that.' Under all the pain, there seemed to be an unspoken question: does loving you stop me from being myself?

Stacey is not alone in finding that her relationship robbed her of her personal identity. 'The rooms of my house seem so crowded. Pets, children's toys, my husband's files when he works at home,' said Barbara, thirty-four and married for fifteen years, 'nothing seems to belong to me. Even the kitchen, which is sort of my space, is constantly being invaded by kids raiding the fridge. If I walk down the street at dusk and look into other people's rooms, they all seem so cool and spacious. Like lighted stages where the owners are people in control, autonomous. I find myself listening to friends who've got divorced and envying their talk of a door of their own.'

Lucy, in her late twenties with a daughter of eight and a son of five, would understand these feelings too: 'There are so many demands on my time. I've had to bottle up the needy part of myself while I've attended to the children. I don't have time for books, so I've put them away and the prospectus from the local college too. But try as I might – because I love my children and my husband – the needy part hasn't shrunk. It wants to smash out and destroy everything.'

Both Barbara's and Lucy's partners were keen to help. Barbara's husband promised to keep his work things tidy and talked about creating an extra room in the loft. Lucy's husband agreed to take the children swimming on Saturday afternoon, so that Lucy could read in peace. But somehow, these well-intentioned plans were sabotaged and nothing really changed.

So what was keeping these couples stuck in the same patterns? We needed to look much deeper than the symptoms: no room for Barbara and no time for reading for Lucy. Both couples told me that they got on well and enjoyed the same things; however, when I asked Lucy for more information, she listed only eating out, cinema, mutual friends and then she petered out. All of these were fine, but they did not invoke any passion from Lucy. In fact, Lucy and her partner, David, had not been to the cinema for six months. When I asked about personal passions, I was met with a blank face. I had to remind Lucy about reading and finally discovered that David used to play golf but had abandoned it when their son was born. Barbara enjoyed interior design – but felt she could not really indulge herself, as she needed to take her husband's tastes into consideration. Now, while compromise is fine – and an essential component for building a relationship – there can be too much compromise.

Both these couples had been so intent on having a happy partnership that they had lost sight of themselves as individuals. No wonder I could not put my finger on their individual interests, because they had been sacrificed – a little here, a little there – to create amorphous couple tastes.

WALKING ON EGGSHELLS

How do you know it is time to talk? A sure sign is the growing tension between negative feelings inside and the superficially pleasant behaviour on the outside. Once someone reaches this stage, they start snapping and their partner feels like he or she is walking on eggshells.

- Do you weigh each word before you say it?
- Does your partner imagine slights when none was intended?
- Does your partner sometimes look at you as if you are the most stupid person on earth?
- Have little things, which never bothered you that much before, started to really irritate?
- Have you become incredibly picky?
- Do you have to keep checking yourself or you'd be exploding all the time?

Answering yes to any of these questions suggests unresolved anger has taken over your relationship. Either your partner is swallowing his or her discontent or you are, or most likely both of you are ducking issues in order to keep the peace. Unfortunately, this strategy has backfired and is making everybody even more miserable. Next time you feel 'got at' or 'at the end of my tether' don't side-step the argument. Instead, let your anger out, have the row, clear the air. Finally, you are ready to discover the underlying causes that have been driving the niggles.

The Six Stages of a Relationship Revisited

Why do some couples become too alike? One of the key ways that a relationship will change, over time, is the attitude to 'difference'. When a couple first start dating, they look for similarities and shared interests. One partner will watch the other compete at a motor cross rally in the pouring rain; the other attends both the dress rehearsal and the performance of their beloved's amateur operatic society.

In the first stage, Blending, all the *differences* are subsumed into becoming a couple. During Nesting, the *differences* start to reappear – perhaps over which shade of paint – and couples no longer pretend that they adore each other's favourite pastimes. However, *similarity* is still more important as a couple build a home together. During Self-affirming, the couple should begin to look at their *differences* because two people will have different tastes, standards, rhythms of getting up and going to bed; the list is endless. Most couples row and end up finding an accommodation for their *differences*.

However, some couples avoid an open confrontation and pretend the *differences* don't exist. One half will drop a hobby – rationalising that there is no time – the other half will stop seeing a particular friend whom their partner does not like. Instead of resenting the decision, this partner will make up an excuse, for example: 'I don't have much in common with my friend any more.' The other tactic for avoiding Self-affirming rows is for a couple to stress *similarities* and to concentrate all their energy on what they have in common.

Alternatively, one partner will start to think, everything would be great if the other partner changed. Locked in this mindset, they think: 'Do it my way and it'll work, because if we do it your way, it won't.' When their partner refuses, they put it down to stupidity, sheer spitefulness or being controlling. Unfortunately, the other partner is probably thinking things would be perfect if only his or her way was adopted. So the rows get bigger and bigger as each partner tries to convince, then cajole, then order the other to 'the right path'. Before long, each partner is stuck, frightened of change and frightened of losing face or their sense of self.

However, without tackling *difference*, it is hard to move on to the next stage, Collaborating, where each partner develops individual projects and brings the new energy back to reinvigorate the relationship. The fifth stage, Adapting, is also tough if a couple pressurise each other into similar opinions and approaches to the multitude of challenges that life throws up.

The final stage, Renewing, is a mirror of the first one. Once again, the couple become everything to each other and *difference* is less of an issue.

Dealing with difference

The diagram on the next page shows what happens to difference from the first date onwards, and how it can undermine a relationship if it is not properly addressed during Self-affirming:

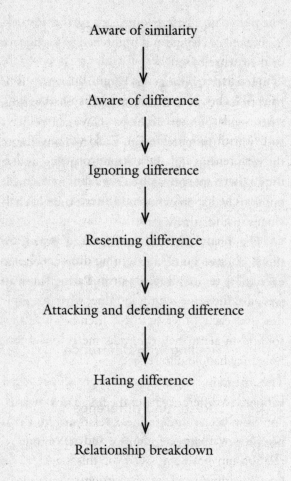

Aware of similarity

↓

Aware of difference

↓

Ignoring difference

↓

Resenting difference

↓

Attacking and defending difference

↓

Hating difference

↓

Relationship breakdown

Ignoring difference

This is why being 'best friends' as opposed to being partners can put a strain on a relationship. We choose friends who are like us and who share similar interests. However, we do not have to live with our friends 24/7, so we can ignore the differences and concentrate on the similarities. What's more, we often have different friends at different life stages as our interests and needs change. The friends who do stay, go through cycles of being very close and then seeing us less often. So, instead of confronting differences, it is easy to let the relationship drift. Partnerships do not have the same luxury. For me, when a couple describe each other as 'best friends', it always sounds an alarm bell that tells me to check out how they handle difference.

Resenting difference

The first warnings of identity and more general relationship problems occur at this stage. A bit like a hairline crack in the sitting-room wall, it does not need immediate attention and might not develop into something serious. Conversely, the crack could mean subsidence and half the house collapsing. So what are the signs that someone is resenting difference? The following would alert my attention: even little plans or decisions have become contentious; one partner is (or both partners are) keeping an imaginary score card on past disputes, and the partners are tiptoeing round each other. The best way out of this trap is to stop ducking the issues and have an argument. Becoming angry releases all the pent-up resentment and the real issues can finally be faced. Often these are different, and frequently less scary, to the ones imagined.

Attacking and defending difference

We all want the best for our partner, don't we? We are happy for them to grow and fulfil their potential. Meanwhile, our partner will do everything to back our ambitions. This is the public face of many relationships. However, underneath, sometimes things are much murkier. Returning to the couples we met at the beginning of the chapter, David understood Lucy's desire to return to full-time education. They had met at university but she had dropped out when she became pregnant. He was happy to pay lip service to her returning – 'one day'. But, in reality, he was attacking her desire to do something different and to be someone other than a wife and mother. He used a classic technique: practical objections. 'I'm really behind Lucy's ambitions, but how are we going to cover looking after the kids? Of course I can help out, but it's more than that,' he explained. 'There're all those hours essay writing and her money from that part-time job isn't just for luxuries.' Every time Lucy would solve one problem, he was ready with another. However, this was more than just a case of a husband trying to keep his wife back. David might have been attacking Lucy's attempts to be different but she too was busy defending the status quo.

In counselling, we had negotiated Saturday afternoons as Lucy's time for some serious reading while David took their children swimming. But week after week, Lucy would find something else that needed doing which prevented her from having even this small amount of time for studying. No wonder they were stuck: both of them were frightened of change. David was frightened that new studies, new friends, new qualifications and new opportunities might mean that Lucy would no longer want him. Meanwhile, Lucy was partly worried about upsetting David, but also about whether she was up to the challenge of being a mature student. Unfortunately, because neither wanted to 'hurt' the other, they had suppressed/failed to confess these feelings. Lucy might have been unhappy, but David was not getting much out of the relationship either. He had been so busy defending the status quo that he had little idea what he wanted for the future. Unable to deal with difference, Lucy and David's relationship was stuck in the stalemate position of 'attacking and defending' and prevented from reaching 'Collaborating' and achieving both of their ambitions.

I'M IN CHARGE/YOU'RE IN CHARGE

Endlessly compromising and trying to second-guess what your partner might enjoy can become boring after a while. A friend had a novel idea for holidays where he would be in total charge for one day and his partner for another. 'I really used to look forward to it,' says Jamie. 'It gave me a chance to get to know Sherrell better. Her suggestions were suffused with her sense of humour and generosity.' Even the children would have their allocated day: 'although that sometimes got a little hairy'. The rest of the holiday would be the usual family compromise. The rules are as follows:

- During your day, you choose all the activities. Beyond something that would completely terrify your partner, the choice is entirely up to you; follow your heart's desire.
- It starts at breakfast and ends at bedtime – what food, where you eat, where to visit, or whether to lie about doing nothing are all up to you.
- Your partner agrees to enter into the spirit of your day and to try, with good grace, to enjoy your choices as much as possible.
- On another day, you swap over and your partner chooses.
- Afterwards, discuss what you have learned about yourself and each other. Ask yourselves: What could we incorporate into our normal routines?
- Before agreeing to this exercise, it is worth having a side discussion about any additional personal rules. Here are a few issues to discuss: does the person in charge have the right to ask for sex? Is there anything that would be totally unacceptable to either one of you?

The exercise can work at home too, with each partner 'in charge' for one day at the weekend or alternate weekends. The same rules as above apply; the only proviso is that the day is devoted to pleasure – a mini-break at home – rather than to catching up on chores and DIY.

Relationship See-saws

One of the best ways of balancing your relationship is to picture yourself and your partner on opposite ends of a children's see-saw. The more that you push down on your side, the more your partner goes up in the air and vice versa. The most comfortable position is where both of you are balanced in the middle, rather than hurtling skywards or downwards. It is the same with arguments. When couples are in crisis, they are nearly always violently see-sawing up and down as each partner tries to take control.

A good example would be Callum and Sinead, both in their thirties, who arrived in my counselling office complaining about their sex life. 'I feel completely unwanted, even though Sinead tells me that she loves me and we care for each other deeply,' said Callum, 'but she doesn't want to touch me. What's wrong with me?' Sinead was equally quick to take the blame: 'It's not you, it's me. I have a low sex-drive.' Instead of

treating their sex life as a shared responsibility –
and a shared problem – they were see-sawing up
and down as first one and then the other took all
the 'blame'. Worse still, the more Callum pushed
down on his side – 'I love you, I want to have
sex, and if we can't sort this out, we don't have
a future' – the more Sinead's desire disappeared
and she flew up into complete abstinence: 'I'm
not interested, not even in masturbation; it's like
you could chop me off at the waist and I wouldn't
care.' Although Sinead did enjoy their monthly
lovemaking, the longer between making love, the
more desperate Callum became until they were
unable to find a middle position where both felt
comfortable.

Here are the most common see-saws. Where do
you sit?

Spender – versus – Saver
*(The more the Spender spends, the more the Saver
needs to save and vice versa; the more the Saver saves,
the more the Spender wants to break out.)*

Emotional – versus – Practical
*(The more the Emotional partner emotes, the
more the Practical partner needs to batten down*

the hatches and vice versa; the more the Practical partner contains, the more the Emotional partner needs to express feelings.)

Extrovert – versus – Introvert
(The more the Extrovert needs company, the more the Introvert retreats and vice versa; the more the Introvert withdraws, the more the Extrovert craves excitement.)

Improviser – versus – Planner
(The more the Improviser leaves everything to the last minute, the more the Planner needs to control and vice versa; the more the Planner controls, the more the Improviser wants to break out.)

Optimist – versus – Pessimist
(The brighter the picture of the Optimist, the more the Pessimist needs to point out the obstacles and vice versa; the more the Pessimist worries, the more upbeat the Optimist becomes.)

How to Balance Your See-saw

These conflicting positions can become so ingrained that it is hard to break free. Here is a step-by-step approach:

- Have a clear picture of what you do want. Often people communicate what they don't want. For example, Callum would say: 'It's not like I want sex five times a day.'

- Tell your partner your picture of how life could be. When Callum explained he would be happy with sex once a week and often he would be just as satisfied with a cuddle, Sinead was relieved. This was close to her picture of their future life together. They had been too busy criticising their partner and defending their own position to communicate what they *did* want.

- Accept that there is no right or wrong. Not only is each viewpoint equally valid, but also our partner puts us in touch with parts of our personality that we overlook or lack. For example, the Spender needs the Saver's restraint (or they would be bankrupt), but the Saver needs the Spender's ability to enjoy their money and life.

- Stop pressing down on your side. This will immediately take you out of the crisis zone. If you slip, remember that the harder you push down at your end, the higher your partner will fly in the opposite direction.

- Instead of trying to convince your partner of the 'rightness' of your position, listen to what he or she has to say. This will allow you to understand the complexity of the issue.

- What's behind both of your views? For example, arguments about money can be about power, security, freedom, dependence and control. When we get particularly angry or upset, there is always something driving the feelings. This can be our fear, past experiences or our personal sense of identity.

- Try and move towards the middle of your see-saw. It will allow your partner to give up his or her extreme position and, in the middle, the ups and downs of disputes are correspondingly smaller. So look for a compromise. Throw out black-and-white solutions and embrace a shade of grey in between.

AUDIT YOUR REACTIONS

This exercise requires nerves of steel, not because it is difficult but because it is very revealing. Next time your discussions seem to be hitting the buffers, switch on a tape recorder. After fifteen minutes, rewind the tape and look out for:

- **Blaming.** These sentences normally start: 'You make me . . .'

- **Placating.** Especially excessive use of 'sorry', 'you're right', 'it won't happen again'.
- **Intellectualising.** Long rambling sentences, which do not seem to go anywhere, is a sure sign.
- **Diverting.** Are both of you truly listening or blocking, contradicting and belittling?
- **How often do you interrupt each other?** This habit will immediately raise the temperature and make reaching agreement harder.

After auditing the conversation, return to the topics discussed and try to cover the same ground again without falling into the same traps.

Summing Up

Doing what we want, and need for ourselves, while continuing to care deeply for our partner is not always easy. However, it can be done by understanding each other's differences rather than by ignoring or protecting against them. Fortunately, secure partners encourage each other to have their own identity because they know this will not undermine the relationship.

IN A NUTSHELL:
- Look for a balance between being one half of a couple and being yourself.
- Find space in your togetherness.
- Too much compromise is as bad as too little.

STEP 6

RE-CALIBRATING

When a relationship has a problem most couples think they need to make a big effort to get big results. Often they vow to try harder and be different: more thoughtful, more open, more helpful around the house – add your own short-comings to the list. For the first few days, both partners follow model behaviour, but of course it cannot last. The result is more bitterness and even depression. So what are the alternatives for re-calibrating your relationship?

A fresh perspective comes not from psychology but from a business book, *The Tipping Point*, in which Malcolm Gladwell writes that 'we have an instinctive disdain for simple solutions. There is something in all of us that feels true answers have to be comprehensive and that there is virtue in dogged and indiscriminate application of effort.'

He goes on to praise the 'Band-aid Solution' (tightly focused and targeted interventions): 'Critics use it as a term of disparagement. But in their history, band-aids have probably allowed millions to keep on working or playing when they would otherwise have had to stop.'

So when relationships are not satisfactory, the answer is not to try harder but just to think smarter. To this end, it is important to understand the laws of change. Gladwell examines how ideas catch on and describes the moment when something crosses over from specialist to mainstream as the Tipping Point. As with a line of dominoes, a small push will ultimately have a big impact. Gladwell claims that 'one imaginative person applying a well-placed lever can change the world'. I thought the theory of Tipping Points might also help explain how relationships can slip almost overnight from 'OK' to 'unhappy'.

In my first interviews with clients, I have always asked when their difficulties started, mainly to find the classic life changes that put relationships at risk: having a child, bereavement, moving house, redundancy, new job and so on. Although these important events make us take stock, they were seldom given as the real cause of a couple's problems. The Negative Tipping Point – where the relationship went from satisfactory to unhappy – seemed to come some time later. However, few couples could pinpoint exactly when this happened. Yet if I asked for reasons why previous marriages or live-in relationships had failed, the majority gave these definite life changes. Could it be that we retrospectively attach big issues to a relationship breakdown, because it makes sense of the big changes in our lives? After all, who would admit to seeking a divorce because of damp towels left on the bed or failing to take the rubbish out?

The Tipping Point theory, however, would suggest that a build-up of what my clients call 'stupid things' are the real causes of marital breakdown. Remember, the key idea is that little things can make a big difference – like, as Gladwell writes, cleaning graffiti from subway trains in New York. More people travelled on the network, and with more passengers around there were fewer muggings, and crime went down dramatically. A virtuous circle had been set up. However, my clients seemed to be trapped in a downward spiral where 'forgetting to load the washing machine' could seed a divorce. So instead of concentrating on major issues, I decided to focus on the little things.

Julia and Graham were in their thirties and their most common argument was about cleaning their young children's shoes. She nagged and he could not understand the fuss. Under this seemingly trivial dispute, we found two further layers. First, Julia's father had always cleaned her shoes and therefore she believed that good fathers did the same. However, Graham had been brought up to be self-reliant and to clean his own shoes. Second, the shoes represented their attitudes to bringing up their children. She wanted to nurture them, while he wanted to make them self-sufficient. Once we had this insight, not only did the shoes cease to be an issue but also the relationship dramatically improved. Instead of being defensive, Julia and Graham began explaining and this knowledge meant better communication, which in turn further increased their understanding. We had begun building a virtuous circle.

Finding Your Tipping Point

There are two key elements for reaching a positive Tipping Point: *the law of the few* and *the stickiness factor*. The first undermines an old myth about relationships: that both halves of the couples have to want to change. Economists talk about the eighty/twenty principle in the market, workplace and wider society. They believe that in any situation roughly 80 per cent of the 'work' will be done by 20 per cent of the participants. Thus 80 per cent of crime is committed by 20 per cent of criminals and 80 per cent of road accidents are caused by 20 per cent of motorists. In other words, a few people have a disproportionate effect on what happens. The same principle applies in relationships. We like to think of them as an equal partnership, but often one half works harder at maintaining the partnership than the other. Many couples arrive in counselling because the partner who used to be responsible for 80 per cent of the relationship glue has given up.

Rosie, a thirty-seven-year-old recruitment consultant, was typical. 'Why should I make all the effort? I kept all the conversation going at mealtimes; I even kept in contact with his mum. But Jake made no effort to fulfil my needs. I felt alone in the relationship, so I just withdrew.' They were stuck, angry and waiting for the other to make the first move. I sympathised with both of them because, in their different ways, they each felt underappreciated. After several weeks, I threw my hands up and asked: 'Do you want to be right or happy?'

Next week they returned with smiles; Rosie had been less critical of Jake and he, in turn, had been more willing to help around the house. They had achieved a positive Tipping Point, but it had required Rosie (the law of the few) to take the initiative. However, she was so pleased that it ceased to matter that she had made 80 per cent of the initial effort because both were now contributing more or less equally.

So why are some messages heard, while others fall on deaf ears? The second law, the stickiness factor, is the answer. Malcolm Gladwell talks about a health trial to make students have tetanus inoculations. Yale University tried various educational booklets – some just informative while others had gory pictures – but the take-up rate remained stubbornly low. However, one small change made 28 per cent of students have the jab: including a map with the health centre ringed and the times of when shots were available. Often tinkering with a message can make it stick. If someone is not listening to us, we find more and more dramatic ways to get their attention – shouting, tantrums, threats, walking out – when often a small change can be far more effective.

Going back to Rosie and Jake, she learned that, by using humour, she could ask for something without coming across as critical. Since discovering *The Tipping Point*, I have spent more time getting clients to 'reframe' their messages to each other rather than forever upping the same ineffective stakes.

When I look back with clients at the end of counselling, often they are astounded by how much was changed by so little. Simon and Tamara are two teachers in their forties. 'Instead of stomping off, I learned to stand up for myself verbally,' says Simon. Meanwhile, Tamara learned almost the opposite: 'I thought I listened, but if he said something I didn't want to hear, I interrupted and effectively shut him up. Nowadays, I've learned to hear him out.' These small but effective changes allowed them to deal more successfully with their major life issues – in this case Tamara's mother's increasingly poor health – without even needing to discuss them in their weekly counselling session. They had dramatically improved their communication skills by one small, key intervention.

FLOP/FLIP TECHNIQUE

When under stress, we have a limited number of ways of responding. For example, we might shout, fly off the handle or go silent. If this does not work, we up the ante: screaming, not speaking for days, or even trashing the house. Soon we are trapped in the same loop with our behaviour getting more and more extreme. Does this sound familiar? Here is a simple trick to break out:

- Next time you're about to launch into your usual response, stop and think: what could I do differently?
- It doesn't matter what. Honestly. Anything is better than the usual response; we know where that leads and that it does not work.
- Try the alternative response and watch your partner's reaction. It will probably make them think too and may prevent him or her from slipping into a standard response.
- If you can't think of an alternative, try the opposite to your normal behaviour. Instead of going quiet, start talking. Instead of throwing ornaments, straighten them. It is amazing how often the opposite behaviour is the key to better communication.
- Remember: stop using the flop response and instead flip it over!

What Stops Couples From Finding Their Positive Tipping Point?

Our attitudes to relationships are underpinned by a set of assumptions that are so fundamental that we take them completely for granted, and therefore rarely check whether or not they are really true. Here are four that could be stopping you from tipping negative into positive:

Nothing I say or do has any impact

When I see a client on their own, because their partner has declined an invitation to join in, they often despair about being able to influence their other half. They feel completely powerless. Melanie, twenty-nine, was convinced of her partner's ability to spoil her day: 'He'll criticise my driving, "You could have got a tank through that space", or he's not phoned when he's going to be late and I'm left in the dark. It's no accident, he knows how to get me riled.' With a little encouragement, Melanie admitted she knew which of his buttons to press too. 'With each meal, Michael puts a small heap of salt on the side of his plate and then keeps dipping his food in it,' she explained. 'If I say anything about how damaging this is to his health, he gets really irritated – which I doubt is good for his blood pressure either.'

If she was aware of the negative buttons to push, surely it follows that she knew the positive buttons to get his cooperation too? 'He loves to be complimented,' she admitted, and agreed to try this strategy. It took a while for Michael to respond – perhaps he was angry or suspected an ulterior motive – but instead of giving up, I encouraged Melanie to keep praising. The results were impressive and soon her and Michael's relationship began to improve.

Although both parties have to be on board to improve a relationship, it only takes one person to start the journey. Pushing positive rather than negative buttons will ultimately create enough goodwill to recruit the second partner into joining the mission. Indeed, Michael started phoning Michelle, not just to tell her if he was going to be late home but also for a general chat.

Breakthrough tip: To get into the mood for pushing the positive buttons, think back to your courting days and what your partner enjoyed. Is there something that you could repeat today?

Me, me, me

This block makes people concentrate on how something impacts on them but forget to make a leap of imagination and consider the effect on their partner. For example, Melanie found it hard to accept compliments from Michael. When he said her new hairstyle suited her, she would shrug it off with a joke: 'At least it looks slimming.' Eventually, Michael stopped giving compliments and Melanie started complaining that he never paid her any attention. So why did Melanie find compliments hard? 'I feel all self-conscious, like I'm the big I AM.' But did she imagine how Michael felt? Finally, she stopped thinking and said quietly: 'When I make a joke of it, he probably feels belittled.'

Breakthrough tip: Next time something upsets you, acknowledge the impact on you – preferably out loud – and then ask your partner how the problem makes him or her feel.

Keep on going to the end of the road

This block is caused by having one fixed idea and continuing to push in that direction – no matter what. When Gavin and Mary started counselling I saw each of them on their own for one session. Unable to cope with conflict, they had simply stopped talking to each other – fearing it would only cause more rows – but instead they ended up with even more misunderstandings. The situation was dire and Gavin despaired for the future: 'I've done everything to build a bridge – I saved up money to buy something special for Mary's fiftieth birthday. I threw a party and invited all her work colleagues, friends and family, but she barely acknowledged me. When I received an inheritance and put all the money into our joint account – to pay off the overdraft – she thanked me, but it didn't make any difference. I don't know what else to do.'

When they started joint counselling, Gavin was determined that they should sort out their finances and brought all the bills and statements along to the session. Although they were back in the red again, Mary side-stepped the money issue and the session went round in circles. Gavin, of course, did not want to provoke an argument so he said nothing and instead kept throwing me dark looks. 'You see, I've tried everything,' he seemed to be saying. For many couples, this is the point where one party, or both, gives up and believes divorce is the only answer. Except that Gavin had not tried everything: he had just kept on going to the end of the road.

Malcolm Gladwell's *The Tipping Point* is full of stories of individuals who made a big change to their community or turned a small business into a multimillion-dollar business – starting what he calls a 'social epidemic'. He writes: 'the world – much as we want it to – does not accord to our intuition. Those who are successful at creating social epidemics do not just do what they think is right.' He goes on to describe how these successful innovators try other avenues – even ones that everybody else would consider counter-intuitive, or even stupid. Gavin's intuition had told him that money was the root of their problems – indeed, they were seriously in debt – and he had tried everything to solve their financial problems. But he had not tried everything to save his marriage. Within a couple of sessions, it became clear that Mary wanted Gavin to talk to her – not about money, but the normal exchange of views and news that make up a day-to-day chat of a happy relationship. Once Gavin started conversing – rather than keeping on to the end of the money road – their relationship tipped into the positive.

Breakthrough tip: If you feel you've tried everything, write a list of this 'everything'. Next, go through the list and cross off all the items that have sent you down the same old road. Finally, think counter-intuitively. What haven't you tried yet?

Old dogs can't learn new tricks

Week after week of counselling, I meet people who are worried that their partner will not change and others who complain: 'She wants me to be something, I'm not' or 'He knew I was like that when he married me'. Yet, week after week, I see that minor accommodations – rather than fundamental shifts in character – will both satisfy the other half's needs and lead to a more fulfilling relationship.

Returning to the couple with the money issues, Mary's fear was that Gavin wanted to change something core to her personality. She believed: 'I work hard and I deserve to treat myself.' (Indeed, it did involve a long commute and work that she found rather tedious.) Mary was convinced that Gavin wanted to turn her from a spender into a saver. In reality, Gavin was worried about how much money went on eating out. 'Restaurants are a waste of money,' he complained. Mary fought back: 'I deserve to be pampered and looked after.'

Ultimately, a compromise was found where Gavin bought the best cuts of meat and all the other trimmings for a wonderful meal but cooked it himself. 'I even put on my best suit and pretended to be the maître d',' he joked. 'You should have seen the look on Mary's face when I showed her to our dining-room table which I had laid with our best tablecloth, cutlery and flowers from the garden.' Mary felt indulged and Gavin was pleased about the money saved. Had they changed? Yes. They stopped going to fancy restaurants (except for birthdays and other special occasions). Were they happier? Most certainly. Had they fundamentally changed each other's personalities? No. Except that this no longer mattered because they had made minor adjustments which had reaped large rewards.

Breakthrough tip: Write down everything that you would like to change about your partner. Next, go back and take the items that are about temperament or personality – which are hard to change – and turn them into specific patterns of behaviour, as these are easier to change. For example, instead of 'be more thoughtful', put 'take me out on Valentine's Day'.

FIND YOUR OWN TIPPING POINT

Often a major change can come from a small internal shift in one or other partner. Here are four small suggestions for re-calibrating your relationship:

1. Be aware of your own internal, self-imposed obstacles. Each partner often waits for the other to commit to improving the relationship. Normally, they have little tests in their mind: 'If he loved me, he'd take more notice of me' or 'If she loved me, she'd show more affection' – except that neither tells the other so the tests remain secret. Instead, be generous, throw away the tests and make the commitment to change.

2. When you wake up, think: 'What is the one thing that I could do today, no matter how small, that could improve my relationship?'

3. Next time you and your partner fall out, try agreeing with them – not for a quiet life but with love and respect. By this, I mean really trying to understand why they hold what seems like a very contrary position. Give him or her the benefit of the doubt; after all, this is someone that you respect and if they hold a position dearly it must have some validity.

4. Whenever you are faced with two choices, always go for the most challenging. Ultimately, the more that you put into your relationship, the more you will get out of it.

Positive Reinforcement

Tipping Points are about finding new ways of looking at things. With a fresh perspective, small changes can lever large ones.

Here is a personal example from dog training which might sound weird, but stay with me. Puppies are extremely exhausting. They have to be watched constantly or they start chewing the legs of the dining-room table that belonged to your great-great-grandmother. Although a puppy wants to please, it does not understand English and has no idea what is good or bad behaviour. I spent so much time telling my puppy 'no' that he probably thought it was part of his name. When I took Flash off to puppy socialisation/dog training, the instructor asked us: 'What do you do when your puppy is lying quietly?' I stuck my hand up: 'Breathe a sigh of relief.' Another class member added: 'Get on with the housework.' Neither of these was the correct answer. 'It's what most people say,' explained the instructor, 'but that's the last thing you should do. How does a puppy know what is good behaviour if you completely ignore him when he does it? What happens when he's been naughty?' We all smiled because we didn't have to answer the question: the puppy got our full attention. 'You're all reinforcing the bad behaviour – with negative attention – and not rewarding the good,' the instructor explained.

From then onwards, if Flash was napping in the sun, I would tickle his tummy and praise him. When he got overexcited and started rushing around the house, I ignored him. At first, I had to consciously think about rewarding good behaviour, because I wanted to use the peace to get on with some writing. But after a few days Flash began to calm down and I soon realised that the extra effort was worth it, and that I was actually saving time by not chasing him around the house.

Here are some tips for using Positive Reinforcement to 'train' your partner:

1. Think back over the past twenty-four hours: how many times did you criticise your partner's

behaviour or nasty habits? How often did you praise? Which came out on top? Positives or negatives?

2. Stop giving negative attention. Instead of complaining, for example, when he watches too much football or she has too many nights out with the girls, wait for the behaviour that you wish to encourage. If your goal is more time together, on your next joint outing, reinforce this positive by telling him or her: 'I'm really enjoying sharing this with you.'

3. Positive Reinforcement is built around compliments and saying thank you. Don't overlook them as nobody can have too many of either.

4. Think of something you appreciate about your partner – but which normally fits into the category of 'goes without saying' – and this time give the thanks out loud. Make the compliment as detailed as possible. Which sounds more heartfelt: 'Thank you for all you do' or 'Thanks for taking my car in to be serviced today, it really made it easier for me'?

Revitalise Your Relationship

Here is an idea which will not only re-calibrate your relationship but will also reawaken passion. Instead of a long lie-in or a romantic meal, do something new that challenges you both. This is because exciting experiences enhance your feelings of attraction towards each other.

The idea comes from a famous experiment over two bridges across a canyon in North Vancouver, Canada. The first was flimsy and wobbled when people crossed it. The sense of danger was enhanced by a large drop on to jagged rocks and rapids below. The second bridge was upstream, steady and low. The researchers got one team of men to cross one bridge and another to cross the other. On the middle of both bridges, they positioned an attractive woman who asked the men to fill out a questionnaire. Afterwards, she told them to call her if they had further questions, and she gave out her home number. The men who crossed the creaky bridge – and whose adrenaline had started pumping – were three and a half times more likely to phone her.

In a further study, two groups of married and dating couples were recruited. One group were given a challenging activity to complete together.

The other had a boring task. The couples who did the exciting activity not only reported increased satisfaction about their relationship but also more intense romantic feelings.

Summing Up

Without challenging deeply held assumptions, a relationship risks continuing down the same old road and you will also be oblivious to any alternative. Sometimes the smallest change can start a positive cycle and tip a relationship from negative to positive. Instead of trying harder, try thinking smarter.

> ### IN A NUTSHELL:
> - Never underestimate the impact of a single generous and open-hearted gesture.
> - Don't wait for your partner to kick-start change, think what changes you could make yourself.
> - If something isn't working, try the opposite approach.

STEP 7

MAINTAINING

It is not only relationships that are under constant pressure – a run of bad judgements can put the future of well-respected high-street stores at risk and public institutions can easily find themselves accused of being 'out of touch'. Providing the same level of service is no longer enough. Competitors get an edge. Customers expect more and more. This is why many businesses champion an idea called the Continuous Improvement Culture. Many schools have also adopted it. The Continuous Improvement Culture suggests that unless something is getting better, it is actually in decline. Therefore management or a head teacher are not satisfied with 'good' but instead strive for 'better'. We need to adopt the same philosophy for our relationships because continuous improvement guarantees that we will not take each other for granted. So how do you achieve this goal?

The Six Special Skills of Successful Couples

Successful couples have, often unwittingly, cultivated six good habits which not only maintain their relationship but also encourage personal growth. I have placed the easiest to adopt first, but the skills build. Like the seven steps, incorporating one habit into your relationship will make the next easier.

Investing

When things go badly a couple will spend more time apart, which breeds even more misunderstandings. Once work, commuting time, sleep and watching TV have been deducted out of a normal week, the average British couple spends little time in each other's company. According to the Office for National Statistics, around three and a half hours a week – or just twenty-four minutes a day – is all that is left for shared social life: sport; hobbies and interests.

Even a small amount of extra time together can pay dividends. Professor John Gottman of the University of Washington proposes an investment of five hours a week to make a profound difference.

Nick and Anna (from the first chapter) tried investing as part of a wider attempt to make their relationship work. Their social life had revolved around their circle of friends. So they reserved one evening a week for each other and, despite friends' tempting offers, this appointment came first. When their night coincided with tickets to a Shakespeare production in the local park, to which their closest friends had already booked them tickets, they came up with a second way of investing. During that particular week they set aside fifteen minutes each evening to chat over the events of the day. Through this kind of small talk, Nick and Anna were able to keep up to date with each other and the important issues emerged naturally. 'This was much better than Nick announcing: "We need to talk",' said Anna. 'That would send me into a panic and make me all defensive.' By prioritising time together, successful couples demonstrate on a daily basis that they treasure their relationship above everything else.

BUILDING NEW HABITS

Many couples start out with good intentions, but after a couple of weeks everything starts to slide. The advantage of habits, over good intentions, is that they build in three key factors for lasting change: *simple events*, which *happen regularly* and can be *easily measured*.

Take, for example, spending more time together. The temptation is to organise a grand gesture – like a cruise or an expensive night out. However, these fail to become habits because, by their very nature, they cannot happen regularly and therefore the benefits quickly fade. By contrast, eating together in the evening can build into a habit. It is definitely *simple*, can *happen regularly* – possibly most weekday evenings – and is *easily measured*. At the end of a month, a couple can look back and check how often they ate together. If this idea appeals, here are some practical tips to reap the benefits of this habit. Don't have the television on or allow other distractions that stop the two of you talking. If one of you gets in much earlier, have a sandwich or something to keep you going. Alternatively, set up a meal together at the weekend – like a long breakfast on Sunday morning – and treat it as a fixed part of your routine.

- What new habits would you like to introduce to your relationship?
- How can you break them down into something *simple*, *repeatable* and *measurable*?
- Think round a new habit, like I have done with eating together, and try to spot any stumbling blocks in advance.

Laughing together

For many successful couples laughter is a tool to knock the edges off a hard day. 'Laughter really does help,' says Elizabeth, a fifty-four-year-old laboratory technician who has been married to Derek, a marketing executive, for twenty-one years. 'We laugh at ourselves, our families, the bizarre habits of neighbours and old movies on the TV. Sometimes it's the only thing that gets us through.' 'We have certain sayings,' explains Derek, 'that would probably mean nothing to anybody else, but I'll tease her that she'll never play for Leicester Ladies Lacrosse again and she'll tell me that the knacker's yard would be too good for me.'

Happily married couples are good at stepping out of an argument for a moment, so that they can make little repairs for their wrongdoings.

A common way of diffusing the moment is to make a joke and this is particularly effective when someone pokes fun at themselves.

DEVELOPING A SHARED SENSE OF HUMOUR

If you and your partner have few opportunities to laugh together – and many couples' social activities are very serious adult activities, like eating out – here are some ideas:

1. A visit to a comedy club.
2. See a funny film at the cinema or a farce at the theatre.
3. Try something difficult like ice-skating together.
4. Do something ridiculous together for charity – like running a three-legged race.
5. Tickle each other.
6. Show each other your baby pictures.
7. Go to the beach and build a sandcastle.
8. Visit a children's petting zoo or a farm.
9. Share something that you haven't done since you were a child.
10. Paint a picture together.

Marrying actions to our words

Only 10 per cent of our communication is with words, but somehow we expect our partners to trust these rather than our behaviour. In the rush of day-to-day living, it is easy to buy off a partner with 'of course I love you' rather than to take the time to show it or act thoughtfully. This is why many couples arrive in couples counselling with one half complaining of being taken for granted. Their partner is often mystified. 'But you know I don't,' is the most common defence. Normally, the complaining half snaps back: 'How?' The conversation grinds to a halt. By comparison, successful couples demonstrate love and appreciation, and perform small acts of caring – the cement that holds a relationship together – rather than just pay lip service.

Many of my clients baulk at this idea of consciously deciding to demonstrate their love, complaining that this would feel artificial. Some feel saying 'thank you' all the time is stupid. Others go further: 'Why should I thank my husband for doing the washing-up? It's not as if they are just my dishes.' On the subject of compliments, these clients worry that being too free will devalue them. With small acts of caring – for example, he irons a blouse for her or she collects him from the station – the fear is that taking over a task, even on just one occasion, is tantamount to having responsibility for it forever. But does it have to be like this?

Successful couples show that really powerful praise, saying thank you or small acts of caring come out of the blue. The occasional: 'Have I ever told you that you've got beautiful eyes?' or 'I really appreciated the way that you rallied round while my mother was ill' will be remembered for a long time. The power of small acts of caring is that they are one-offs. It is always more effective to *show* your partner your deep affection than just to *tell* them about it.

The art of compromise

Instead of having winners and losers, or unbalanced power, successful couples find a middle way. An example would be sharing out household duties according to who has the time. When chores are rigidly divided, there are often niggling resentments. Compromise is very different from compliance – just giving in – in that partners will put their viewpoint strongly and maybe even fight for it. However, rather than digging in and never giving ground, successful couples will look for a middle ground. This is corroborated by the findings of Professor John Gottman. The best predictor for which couples, studied in his laboratory, stayed married was how well they argued and resolved their differences. This turned out to be more important than either the type of issue faced or even the severity.

David and Simone, two teachers who had been together five years, learned to compromise but only when they were heading for a break-up. Although the couple had few fights, both partners had entrenched positions. David was keen on hang-gliding but Simone felt that it took him away too often and did not leave them with enough couple time. Generally, David went once a month and Simone patrolled this tradition – in case hang-gliding ate into more weekends. When David's hang-gliding club proposed a long weekend away, Simone put her foot down and they had a series of nasty fights. 'David doesn't get much holiday and we like to use what there is for a decent break,' Simone explained. However, Simone chose to be generous: 'I decided to stop going on at him about hang-gliding because it was casting such a big shadow over our lives. He knew how I felt and it was pointless going on about it.' Ultimately, Simone had a nice surprise. 'David didn't really go hang-gliding that much any more, just the occasional special opportunity and it stopped being an issue.' David added: 'With the atmosphere being much better at home, I've been getting away from the office earlier and spending more time with Simone. It's funny, but I found that I had been defending "me" time and really there was no need.'

Both Simone and David discovered they had been fighting over an arbitrary line in the sand. Their new compromise worked better, each of them felt more relaxed and their relationship flourished.

FIVE USEFUL SUBJECTS TO ARGUE ABOUT

The best way to bond is to have a good argument. It gets all the issues out in the open, provides a release of pent-up feelings, and a sense that the relationship can get better.

1. **Little things**

   Small irritations such as stacking the dishwasher badly may not seem like serious crimes, but they can cause huge resentment if not dealt with. Also, if you find conflict especially difficult, these smaller issues can provide a dry run before tackling something really contentious.

Breakthrough tip: Bring up your niggle at the time – rather than a couple of hours later when it's too late for your partner to do anything about it. Don't hide behind a joke because your partner will wonder if you really mean it. Also avoid slowly building up to the request with statements like 'You're not going to like this' or 'There's something I need to bring up' – which will put your partner on the defensive. Just ask directly.

2. **Amount of time spent together**

   With so many demands on our time, it is easy to put our partner at the bottom of the list. But if Loving Attachment is not nurtured, it withers, so ring-fence time together.

   Breakthrough tip: Don't fall into the trap of concentrating on, for example, the amount of time your partner spends outside the house or on hobbies – this just invites a justification of his or her behaviour or a dispute about the facts. Instead, discuss how this makes you feel. For

example: I feel neglected/taken for granted/
not important. As you are the expert on your
feelings, this is harder to contradict.

3. **Different tastes**

Differences make things more interesting,
highlighting your role as partners rather than
as best friends or twins. Choose something
in the news or a movie you have both seen,
and discuss it together. Standing up for your
views is not only healthy, but you will also
probably learn something new about each
other. These arguments can even take on
a playful tone and present an opportunity
for mock fighting – very useful if you find
confrontation difficult.

Breakthrough tip: Always have an opinion. If
you opt out, 'It's OK, you choose what we will
do this weekend', your partner will feel 100 per
cent responsible for the success of an outing,
which can become very wearing.

4. **Money**

Arguments about money are harder to negotiate but provide an express route to important,

but often hidden, issues. Money can stand for power, self-respect, freedom, responsibility, security and even love. So when you discuss money, be aware that you're not just talking about pounds and pence, and try to delve deeper.

Breakthrough tip: Get your partner to talk about what money meant when they were growing up. Next, share the lessons you have learned from your childhood. This will help you see your differences through fresh eyes and discover room for compromise.

5. **Sex**

This is another tough area but one that can pay real dividends. Whether the arguments start with 'You don't fancy me any more' or 'Why do you always push me away', it will bring into the open deeper issues that many couples are too embarrassed to discuss.

Breakthrough tip: Be extra considerate. Instead of blaming: 'You make me feel . . .', own the problem: 'I feel . . .' This will stop the argument becoming unnecessarily confrontational.

Taking risks

When we first fall in love, Limerence provides a magic cloak of omnipotence that blinds us to the risks of starting a new relationship. However, once Limerence wears off, each partner will start defending themselves and putting up barriers. However, successful couples continue to take small risks (like upsetting their partner) and bigger ones (like one partner retraining and meeting a lot of new people). With many couples who have been through a rocky patch, the decision to take a risk is nearly always a sign that the relationship is on the mend. Rita fell out of love with her husband, Joe, after nineteen years and three children together. Since she came clean about her true feelings, Joe had been even less likely to rock the boat. 'My policy is to stress the positive,' he told me at our first counselling session.

However, as we worked through the seven steps, he became bolder. 'We were out shopping and she took my hand, after months with no physical contact, and I wanted to know why,' Joe explained. 'Normally I would have kept my mouth shut, in case I heard something I didn't want to hear or maybe she would take her hand away.' This time Joe took a risk and told Rita how much he enjoyed the contact. 'I told him it just felt right to hold his hand,' said Rita, 'and later we had a long conversation over coffee. I hadn't meant the hand-holding as some grand gesture but the more we talked, the more important this impulse seemed.'

Another example of someone taking risks is Amy, a twenty-six-year-old singing teacher, who was offered a contract to work in France. Her initial response was to turn it down. 'It involved four months in Paris and although I liked the picture of me sitting at a pavement café in Saint-Germain-des-Prés,' she explained, 'it would mean being apart from Alan.' The idea of being stuck at home, while his partner had an adventure, did not appeal much to Alan either. 'If I was honest,' he admitted, 'I could picture her being swept off her feet by a sophisticated Parisian.' However, Alan decided it was best to give Amy his blessing and she took the job. The Eurostar train link allowed them to spend 50 per cent of their weekends together, Alan took some holiday in Paris and learned French too. 'I could really get into the way of life over there,' he said, 'buying fresh croissants and *pain au chocolat* for breakfast. The quality of the ingredients for cooking was an eye-opener.' Ultimately, Paris became an adventure to share together, and Amy's contract an opportunity to grow together rather than a threat. Both falling in love and maintaining love involves taking a risk, because without risk there is little learning or growth.

Allowing each other to be different

Successful couples allow each other freedom to grow – even if this means doing things without each other. At the other end of the scale are couples who lean on each other to the extent that one, or both, fears they would collapse without an all-encompassing togetherness. Most couples sit somewhere in between these two positions, but at times of challenge most of us are likely to veer towards controlling or clinging.

The importance of some degree of independence has been underlined in the study of lesbian couples. Women have the reputation for being keen on intimacy and good at it. In theory, therefore, lesbian relationships should be extremely stable. In 1983, American sociologists Philip Blumstein and Pepper Schwartz interviewed 4,314 heterosexual couples (both married and cohabiting), 1,875 gay couples and 1,723 lesbian couples. They returned eighteen months later and found the couples least likely to break up were the married heterosexuals (14 per cent had split), followed by cohabiting heterosexuals (29 per cent) and then gay couples (36 per cent), but most likely to break up were lesbians at a startling 48 per cent.

So what made the lesbian couples least likely to stay together? This was the task that Susan Johnson, University of Wisconsin, set herself in her book: *Long-term Lesbian Couples* (1990). She gave questionnaires to 108 lesbian couples across 21 states, who had been together for 10 years or more, and followed up many with an interview. At the beginning, she thought the high split-up rate could be caused by the pressures on lesbian couples, and the lack of support from mainstream society; although gay couples face the same problems. Her second theory was that lesbian couples were too quick to consider themselves couples – hence the old joke: what does a lesbian bring on a second date? Answer: a removal van.

When Johnson completed the research, she found her preconceptions had been wrong. Successful lesbian couples were prepared to allow each other to be different but the lesbians who had split expected their partners to have a similar take on life. 'You may think you are living as part of the same relationship, but you're not,' Johnson wrote about her own relationship. 'My partner says ours is the easiest relationship she has been in;

I say no, for me it is the hardest. For a long time we argued about who was right. It took us several years to realise we're not in the same relationship. She is living with me, one experience, and I am living with her, a very different experience.'

All couples like the idea of their partner being the same: having the same experiences; interpreting reality the same; coming to the same conclusions. However, this is not only impossible but also probably undesirable. Sameness is fine but equally important is an awareness of the differences, so each partner can create a clear space for themselves as individuals within a relationship too. This is why independence – both in the physical sense of being apart from time to time and in the intellectual sense of being allowed to have different thoughts and come to different conclusions – is so important.

The couples interviewed by Johnson for her study of lesbian relationships sum up an important point and offer sound advice. One woman said: 'There is no such thing as a relationship without conflict. You have to have some kind of acceptance of that; it just ain't gonna happen. Another person is not the answer. There ain't nothin' out there that is perfect.' Nearly all the couples in Johnson's book had been through some crisis that could have split them up. May, in an eighteen-year-long relationship, was typical: 'I think sometimes – this sounds silly, but I think it's true – people don't hang in long enough to know that you live past it [the crisis]; it does not have to be this big gaping wound, it can heal. People aren't patient enough.'

Summing Up

None of our myths is stronger than 'love conquers all', but this is only part of the story – determination, courage and investing time are equally important. *Investing* will encourage a couple to start *Laughing together*. *Marrying actions to our words* will create the goodwill for *The art of compromise*, which, in turn, makes *Taking risks* easier and, ultimately, *Allowing each other to be different* is in sight.

> ### IN A NUTSHELL:
> - Make certain that there is joy in your relationship.
> - A commitment to continual learning will both renew your relationship and keep it on track.
> - A life-long affair does not stand still, it keeps getting better and better.

FINAL NUTSHELLS

1. Lifting the Lid

- There are two equally unhelpful myths about love.

- The first claims true love lasts for ever and that once soulmates find each other, all problems melt away. Unfortunately, this overlooks the impact of real life plus the energy, skills and commitment needed to make love work.

- The second celebrates the magic of falling in love but expects daily life to drain away the passion, cites the high divorce rates and thinks the best we can hope for is a series of short-term affairs.

- The truth lies somewhere in the middle of these two myths. It is possible to build a life-long love affair but only if we understand love, how it changes over time and what is needed for it to endure.

- After all, unless we understand love, it is impossible to let our partner know what we need.

Checkpoint: Find the positive angle. Unfortunately, many people communicate in negatives. For example: 'We don't go out any more.' Their partners become defensive, justify themselves or switch off. However, if you put the same thought into a positive – 'I really enjoy it when we go out together' – your partner will feel complimented, committed and ready to please.

2. Diagnose Potential Problems

- There are six stages of love, each with its own challenges and special rewards.
- The problems arise when we expect love and each other to remain the same, preserved in aspic, rather than allowed to grow and change.
- If you follow the six stages, love grows stronger. The couples who have been together the longest are the most romantic.
- At the beginning, love is based on the promise of a life together; later it is built on the reality of a life shared.

Checkpoint: Take an interest in your partner's life. He or she will feel truly cherished, especially if you are there for every aspect of his or her life – not just the parts of which you approve or particularly enjoy. So go along and watch the finals of his five-a-side competition or help set up her adult education class's exhibition of craft work.

3. Improve Your Communication

- Couples who can talk over a problem and listen attentively to the other's position can overcome any challenge.
- It is impossible for two people to live together without disagreements.
- Learn to argue with respect (praising each other's good points, maintaining good eye contact and looking for solutions where everyone has a benefit).
- Avoid arguing with disrespect (jumping to conclusions, expecting your partner to be a mind-reader and counter complaining).

Checkpoint: If your partner has a strongly held opinion, there must be an important reason why he or she feels like that. Instead of dismissing these opinions as wrong or misguided, discover why your partner feels so passionately. Listen to the explanation, ask questions to be sure that you really understand and repeat back your conclusions (to check that they are right). If you give your partner this consideration, he or she will be more likely to hear you out too.

4. Boost Intimacy

- True intimacy depends on equality as it is hard to be open with someone we feel will control or judge us.
- If someone feels powerless – for real or perceived reasons – it frequently translates into a low sex-drive.
- Men often use sex to get close. Women usually need to be close to have sex.
- Good loving needs acceptance and trust.
- Don't be afraid to mix things up by finding new places to make love (like the bathroom or lovers' lane) and bringing new things into the bedroom (like massage oils or dressing up).

Checkpoint: Set aside intimate time. Instead of waiting until both of you are in the mood and not tired, which probably happens less often than you would wish, plan ahead and put a date in your diaries. Make certain there is enough time to relax, put on some music and slow dance together, give each other a long massage and have a cuddle. Agree that it does not have to end in sex – because it is about being physically intimate together – and all the pressure to 'perform' will be removed.

5. Balancing You and Me

- We need both to be ourselves and to be loved. Unfortunately, there can be an unspoken message in a relationship: If I don't like what you do, I won't love you any more.

- There are two competing fears in every relationship. On the one hand, we worry about being trapped and suffocated by our partner. On the other, we worry about being abandoned and alone in the world.

- It is very easy to blame our beloved for making us unhappy or driving us to the extremes of being clinging or needing space. However, it is more constructive to look at our own behaviour and how it contributes to the problem.

Checkpoint: Take the plank out of your own eye first. It is very easy to justify our own thoughtlessness or selfishness. Try extending the same privileges to your partner and re-examine their behaviour through this forgiving lens. How could you build bridges between the two of you?

6. Re-calibrating

- The constant demands of children, family, friends and work often make us put our relationship last. Because our partner loves us, we believe we can take them for granted. Up to a point, this is true.

- However, unless a relationship is nurtured, it will wither and die.

- We imagine that we should make grand gestures – exotic holidays or expensive meals – but lots of small ones are equally effective and create good habits.

- Think every day: what small thing can I do today to make my partner feel appreciated? It could be sending a text, buying a bar of their favourite chocolate when you fill up with petrol or telling them that you love them.

Checkpoint: We find it really difficult to give compliments. Maybe you didn't get compliments as a child – because your parents were frightened of making you big-headed? Maybe praising your partner makes you uncomfortable – perhaps he or she might think you're after something. Whatever the reason for not praising, there is a danger that your partner will feel taken for granted. Make a resolution to try and say thank you, or give a compliment every day. Although this might feel forced to start off with, it will soon become second nature.

7. Maintaining

- Love cannot be taken for granted. It takes continued investment of time, energy and commitment.
- Respect is the greatest gift that you can give your partner. All partnerships go through phases of questioning their love for each other. However, if you still respect each other, the relationship will emerge safely out the other side.
- Marriage, like water, always finds it own level. In good relationships we match up with

someone with a similar intelligence, talent and looks. So in respecting our partner, we are also respecting ourselves.

Checkpoint: Keep things fresh. Once a week try and do something different. It might be sitting down and watching your partner's favourite TV show with him or her, arranging a surprise trip to the theatre together, or doing something out of character.

FINAL NUTSHELL:

- Although falling in love is a magic experience, relationships grow stronger and deeper over time as they put down roots based on trust, commitment and compassion.
- A love that has been tested and has survived will always be sweetest, so embrace your problems and learn from them.
- A life-long love affair is within your reach.

A Note on the Author

Andrew G. Marshall is a marital therapist and the author of *I Love You But I'm Not In Love With You: Seven Steps to Saving Your Relationship*, *The Single Trap: The Two-step Guide to Escaping It and Finding Lasting Love* and *How Can I Ever Trust You Again?: Infidelity: From Discovery to Recovery in Seven Steps*. He writes for *The Times*, the *Mail on Sunday*, the *Guardian*, *Psychologies* and women's magazines around the world. His work has been translated into over fifteen languages. Andrew trained with RELATE and has a private practice offering counselling, workshops, training days and inspirational talks.

www.andrewgmarshall.com

THE SEVEN STEPS SERIES

ARE YOU RIGHT FOR ME?
Seven steps to getting clarity and commitment in your relationship
ISBN 9781408802625 · PAPERBACK · £6.99

*

HELP YOUR PARTNER SAY 'YES'
Seven steps to achieving better cooperation and communication
ISBN 9781408802632 · PAPERBACK · £6.99

*

LEARN TO LOVE YOURSELF ENOUGH
Seven steps to improving your self-esteem and your relationships
ISBN 9781408802618 · PAPERBACK · £6.99

*

RESOLVE YOUR DIFFERENCES
Seven steps to coping with conflict in your relationship
ISBN 9781408802595 · PAPERBACK · £6.99

*

BUILD A LIFE-LONG LOVE AFFAIR
Seven steps to revitalising your relationship
ISBN 9781408802557 · PAPERBACK · £6.99

*

HEAL AND MOVE ON
Seven steps to recovering from a break-up
ISBN 9781408802601 · PAPERBACK · £6.99

ORDER YOUR COPY:

BY PHONE: +44 (0)1256 302 699;

BY EMAIL: DIRECT@MACMILLAN.CO.UK

ONLINE: WWW.BLOOMSBURY.COM/BOOKSHOP

WWW.BLOOMSBURY.COM

BLOOMSBURY